A Season on the Earth

Selected Poems of Nira█

A Season

on the Earth

Translated by *David Rubin*

COLUMBIA UNIVERSITY PRESS

NEW YORK

1976

This volume is sponsored by the Asian Literature Program of The Asia Society, New York. Some of these translations have appeared previously in *Hudson Review* and *Poetry East West;* they are used here by permission.

UNESCO COLLECTION OF REPRESENTATIVE WORKS
INDIAN SERIES

This book has been accepted in the Indian Series of the Translations Collection of the United Nations Educational, Scientific and Cultural Organization (UNESCO)

Columbia University Press
New York   Guildford, Surrey

Book designed by Eric Sackheim

Library of Congress Cataloging in Publication Data
Tripathi, Surya Kant, 1896–1961.
A season on the earth.

(Unesco collection of representative works : Indian series)
I.   Rubin, David George, 1924–   II.   Title.
III.   Series.
PK2098.T7A27   891 ′.43 ′15   76–40026
ISBN 0–231–04160–8
ISBN 0–231–04161–6 pbk.

Translator's Dedication

To Oppi and Saara Untracht

rakkaudella

Contents

Foreword

There is still considerable mystery surrounding many circumstances in the life of the great Indian poet known as Nirala (1899?–1961). The meaning of some passages throughout his work and even his sanity, along with many biographical details, such as the exact date of his birth, are matters of continuing dispute. To describe Nirala's role and his importance in modern Hindi literature requires a somewhat detailed consideration of the literary and linguistic background from which the poet emerged. But since it is my hope that Nirala's poetry itself will command the chief interest of most Western readers of this book I have accordingly reserved a general survey of Nirala's life and work, in the form of an afterword, along with some remarks on the translation, for the end of the book.

Nirala was extremely fond of short lyrics describing the various Indian seasons, a tradition that can be traced back to classical Sanskrit literature as well as to Prakrit and vernacular poetry. For his own anthology of his work up to 1950 Nirala chose the title "*Aparā*," the experience (or wisdom) of the world and hence the contrary of transcendental. There is doubtless an ironic overtone in this designation, for Nirala apparently believed, like the Madhyamikas and some Vedantins, that the physical universe, though it may be termed ultimately unreal, is nevertheless the vehicle of revelation of the absolute reality and, even, not to be distinguished from it by an enlightened awareness. In inventing a title for this collection of translations of Nirala's work I have sought to suggest these elements of the "worldly" or earthly life and the transitory and cyclical character of the physical universe.

The translator wishes to express his appreciation to Shri S. P. Nirash of Delhi University, Mr. Asad Rahman and Mrs. Shaista Rahman of Brooklyn College, Dr. Vasant Joshi of the University of California in Berkeley, and Shri Vishnu Khare, the Hindi poet, for their many valuable suggestions regarding Nirala's language and style; to the American Council of Learned Societies for the fellowship making possible the research in India for this book; to Mrs. Bonnie R. Crown, Director of the Asian Literature Program of the Asia Society, and Miss Andrea Miller, Assistant Director, for their constant encouragement and support in completing this work; and to Shri Ramakrishna Tripathi, Nirala's son, and to Lokbharti Publishers and Bharati Bhandar of Allahabad for their kind permission to publish these translations.

A Season on the Earth

1. Poetry and the Poet's Life

To a Friend

1.

You* say, "Leave off
    that insipid singing,
What meter's in it,
    what life, what feeling?
Once the lake overflowed,
echoing calls of cranes and swans,
water-giving cloud and lotus
water-born, to mutual love
compelled. The waves made music,
and the banks resounded like drums;
among the swings the artful breeze
        sang *rāg* Malhar."**

2.

It's true, friend,
    true: no buzz
of life there,
    not a croak, not a grunt.
Here all eight watches of the day
the wind worries its way along
and the heat scorches all places.
        Every drop of water evaporated,
        the once full ponds dried up,
        the green branches crackling
        and alas both peacock and snake***
        linked by their tails.

3.

At this same time we saw
    visions of many kinds,
green places shimmering
    in this same heat.
The bees hovered distracted
over the fresh leaves and buds,
ready to die for those little bodies
    but frustrated time and time again.
That soft fragrance
    which spread enchantment—
did it not reach you, friend?
    did your door stay shut?

4.

At this same time the mango bent,
    its branches heavy with fruit—
did you not find it when
    you looked out on creation?
    Did you not hear one note
    of the hymn of praise within it?
    A sorry fate—for you,
    friend, it was only heat.
Shut too your ears,
deaf to the sounded fifth,*
    on your spirit the old seal,
    and a stone on your heart.

5.

Try to remember what it was,
        the holy feeling that freed you
of all divisions, all distinctions,
        and bound friend to enemy. You
alone turned away, remained alone,
fool, leaving your beloved friend.
Tell me, what rivalry can be
        where there's union, where there's love?
If you cling to this form,
stay steeped in this existence,
how will you get across
        the uncrossable dark sea?

6.

The fierce wind blew, friend—
        it could not be stopped.
Tired, you looked on
        and untiring it blew.
Did you understand those early years?
—pleasures free, unhindered,
the violent tensions of the young
        at war with all control.
Overhead the noonday heat
seared and hissed. Bending
and shaking trees innumerable
        that fierce wind blew.

7.

The force that drove you on
     has long since spent itself.
And tell me, when was burned-out fire
     made to flame again?
Those old withered leaves,
shriveled, giving no shade,
scattered on the ground—
you were attached to them
by love immeasurable, and savorless.
And thus you found
     suffering without a cause.

8.

The wind blew, bursting
     all futile bonds of verse,
blew sounding a lament
     for all recurring cycles.
In the room at midnight
you took your rest,
or fabricated delightful worlds
     from worlds long dead.
And the wind wandered ceaselessly
here and there on false-leading desert paths,
burning away the marks of grief,
giving everything the color
     of the ashoka tree.*

9.

The wind found rest nowhere,
nowhere found a place to halt,
compelled on blindly,
    journeying on the sea.
Waves suddenly crested high
in countless billows,
blue bodies plunging
    frantic with desire.
Even there the wind destroyed:
finding the ship in dire distress
it turned her over in the storm
    before she could reach the shore.

10.

It calmed today, the wind
    and the heart in the breast.
So, friend, no anguish,
    no cries for help.
The atoms which flew up in wind
descend now as beneficent rain,
and gleam like pearls*
    in the heart of the shell.
Look! Who's made
    this necklace of poems
and strung it on the breast
    of Sarasvati**, dazzling
    his eyes with his reflection?

(1935)

It's True

It's true,
this is the gift you gave:
the pride in serving Hindi,
the first-hand knowledge of the people—
and this is also the real blessing.
It's true.

Defeated time and time again
I sought new defeat in the ashes.
The dust has gone flying, filled the whole body.
Not a blossom: life hasn't opened—
it's true.

(1935)

Letter to the Flowers of Hindi

Today
my beauty's wilted, blighted,
and you put forth fine scent and hue and leaf.
I'm trampled under foot
and you are casual monarch over all.

Though I too am a messenger of spring
I do not envy you,
as like an untouchable among a host of Brahmans
I sit apart.

Much lauded majesty you are,
flowering from the tree's heart.
I—a letter thrown away when read,
and you fresh nectar for every bee.

But see—what many-savored juice
is in the fruit you bear
once it has left your heart and ripened—
of what use to the tree?

They say the best fruit's hard to reach.
You only play with baubles
if you renounce the bitterness at its core.
As for me, my critic is a seed.*

(1937)

Only One Madness

Only one madness:
neither the passion of youth
though unrestrained as youth alone,
nor the sadness of childhood
though restless as childhood alone.
Nor did he find in it the music
to sing for a lifetime
nor the bitter renunciation
that lets one forget a moment
the sense of self.
For him, acute suffering;
for others, a game;
a life like a bird's,
joyous—but for pitiless children,
without love.
Unadorned poetry flowed, unstoppable,
as from some poet's throat
an endless stream of flowers.
The slanderous crowd buzzed—but far.
For when had he ever time to listen?
Ecstatic
he never saw in it a sadness,
saw only one madness.*

(1922)

Poem

She sat on a rock,
her blue skirt gently fluttering—thus,
uninhibited, the evening breeze
held some silent conversation with the lovely girl
and smiled.
Her curling hair,
black and luxuriant,
blew loose and fragrant over her pale face,
tumbled over her breasts,
teased her affectionately.
From the open sky
the chill spray scattered,
exhilarating,
on her shapely limbs.

This was the whole poem,
her charms and her adornment
its only imagery.
If those vina strings gave forth no music
surely that was entirely the poet's failure.
He made only a pathetic cry:
"To describe her I devised a style
but the venture alas proved useless."
His heart and the poem's heart
were filled with love.
But she was innocent, guileless.
From her every limb there rose vibrations—
they reached the poet, told him,
"Come over,
she's calling you to cross,
quickly, to the other side."

(before 1930)

River Crossing

The boat drifts, the current's fierce—
steer well, boatman of my life.
Skimming, turning
in the churning waves
the boat is swamped,
faltering, halting
on the waters.
Shaking, quaking,
it comes about,
the rudder broken—
boatman of my life!
I'm gripped by fear,
struck with trembling
through and through.
Second by second
the flood is rising.
Infinitely far
the other shore,
boatman of my life.

(1920)

Hopeless

Life:
    a wailing and a bawling
        without end.
My own heart's tough as steel—
    you can pound it for all it's worth.

Let
    the dawn light never rise
    on the blind night
        of my sorrow;
    there won't be light enough
        nor praise, nor welcome.

Let
    my prayers be
        unanswered;
    every petal of the heart's lotus
        blighted;
    life
        shot.

Let
    my soul
    created in emptiness
    take to itself the emptiness
        of creation.

Let
    my world
        go down.
            Even then
      in that vast dark
    my ramshackle wagon
will go lurching on.

                        (1927)

A Stump

Today a stump,
its power gone,
all foliage gone.

No longer does it quicken with the spring
nor sprouting green bend like an archer's bow
nor shoot out the love god's blossomed arrows;
no travelers sit sighing in its shade,
nor any pair of lovers shedding tears.

Only one old bird
sits there, remembering a little.

(1937)

A Look at Death

What I've not said, say now,
you ever-youthful goddess,
create and yet again create your songs.
In a world too vast
you locked me in
and humbled me with grief.
And what you say is:
        "Through sorrow's workings
        I've granted you new riches.
        Transform those bird's wings now,
        in the water become a fish;
        the free sky's gone, so let
        existence in the sea
        suffice."
Clear, everything you said to me,
and still I didn't understand,
and that caused all my suffering.
That loving kiss you gave to me
today's a cup, brimming with poison.
And you laugh and tell me, "Drink, my lover,
my desperate lover, drink. Freedom am I!
In death I come.
Fear not."

(1938)

The stream of love has run dry.
Like sand the body left behind.

This mango branch that looks dried out,
it says, "They come to me no more,
the peacock and the cuckoo. I am a written line
without a meaning,
      the life burnt out of me.

"I gave my blossom and my fruit to the world,
dazzled it with my splendor; and thought
each greening moment had to last forever—
such was the very structure of that life
      that's crumbled."

"My darling comes to me no more
to linger gorgeous on the dark green grass.
Mere darkness pours over my heart.
I am lost to sight."
      This is what the poet said.*

(1942)

Wild Jasmine

Beginning of the year:
flowering breasts of the earth—
the hills high in their beauty;
behind the new leaves
bees and koels, their lives all vibrancy of sound,
create a music of desire
that rouses joy, fires up
the fiercest youthful craving.
The potent, dazzling sun
a hundred times kisses the kissed earth
with wild rays beyond the counting,
greedy, ferocious, tender, lustful,
his eyes the equitable eyes of love,
giving all gifts
and taking in return
the beloved's own freely given pride.
More and more terrible
the heat burns,
the earth sweating and trembling
as though her lover stroked her breasts,
her eyes shut in ecstasy,
her moan the scorching wind.
And in that wind all creatures and all matter
alike insensate.

Tonight the sky
took on the look of doom,
sulphurous, overwhelming conflagration,
smokeless, cloudless, swamping everything,
turning the universe to ash, save for oneself.
Dust rose, the land beneath it disappeared.
Slowly, in my own frustration sadly taking in the scene,
I walked down toward the river, and I thought;
"My life's a total waste.

I've lost the battle.
I never dreamed that everyone
would beat down all my aspirations—"
and much more of the sort.
Reaching my favorite spot
I sat alone there, watching,
full of an aching music.

Then I began to muse some more along that line:
"If I had been some prince's son
I wouldn't suffer these disgraces.
Just think how many scholars would be my hangers-on,
heads bowed and hands stretched out for my largesse.
I'd give a little—and take much more.
And all the papers—unanimously!—would chant my praises.
My life story would provide the feature articles—
lavishly illustrated, you may be sure.
Not only that. As the heir of a millionaire
I'd be educated far beyond the Arabian Sea.
My father—what an expert on the morals of the nation!
with a firm grip on his money and—not batting an eyelash—
a fervent Communist as well, preaching the Revolution;
and the people—how carefully they'd think it through!—
would elect him President.
Ten national songs (for a fee) would honor him,
and they'd sell them, singing them in tones
harsher than any jackass's.
And not to be left behind, the Hindi societies
would pronounce them (lest they perish first) immortal.
When the news was flashed to me by cable
what banquets I'd give the lordlings,
the sprees we'd go on—and in this fashion
I'd manage to lay out a mere six thousand per month.
Then—my education completed—back to my worthy old man.
I'd step down delicately from the plane,
producing a great effect in the press.
They'd all come running, camera in hand,
hastily getting in their requests,
which graciously I'd accord them.
I'd pose in various stances,

in aspects of some twenty moods, looking up or down.
And then I'd give the country my message,
stern and moving, in which
only the language would be the country's.
I'd dish up all the new Russian ideas,
which only the sharpest would comprehend
after they'd read them over and over again.
Then with my father I would swear
a solemn oath to serve the people,
and standing on a podium I'd proclaim
the benevolent Bolshevik line."

With heat the summit of the evening sky
had turned red, reddening the whole horizon.
Troubled, I opened my eyes, looked eagerly,
for it seemed as though a balmy fragrance drifted
from the beloved's hair. At once I thought:
I came here alone and I've sat here alone.
Then turning I saw all around me the smiling jasmine,
its own life filled with that heat,
taking heat and tribulation on its head,
breathing up an infinite sigh from the depths,
like the devotion of a sage that pierces through
the weaved-up suffering of earthly life,
rising serene,
or as a lovely apsara
crosses over the sea of foaming milk,
limbs and hair drenched from myriad waves,
and trembling under the arrow-eyes
of the astonished world.
I said, "Jasmine, no one suspects
that you bloom here, spilling out your music.
When the fierce heat strikes
you create a wine in your little chalice,
and you fill it with the coolness of the underworld."
Head bowed respectfully, I drew closer.
Suddenly the evening breeze rose, carrying
the fragrance of the vine with bending, tensing, laughing gusts.
Then the jasmine turned its face with its known-forever look,
every moment pouring forth the pure scent of its body,

and said, "I give everything.
Don't touch me. You forget your place,
your touch has become impure. Look from afar."
I stopped there on the path
Which shone bright in the glow
of a new liquid light,
and I praised the vine:
Radiant tender forest girl,
what poetry can claim such milk-white petals?
Where else such constant love
or such a garland on the breast of worldly lovers?
What heroine has this easy rhythmic grace
or such bewitching fragrance in her kissed tresses?

"Only yourself you've wasted, only played
in this life," said the jasmine.
its body shivering.
"Ku-u ku-u," the koel sang in ultimate bliss,
"Lover where lover where?" the papiha's amorous voice*
that spreads sweet poisoned feelings in the breast.
The wind rose, stirring every greening leaf,
the river flowed, its waves a-tremble
and full of longing, and the stars unparalleled
wandering in the sky-darkness spied out
the jasmine's loveliness—their light the light
of thousands of astonished eyes.
Overwhelmed, I watched; the wild jasmine laughed,
spoke with indiscernible tones:
"The carnival of this world glitters
only with the shallow beauty of things
that turns the treasure of the soul to stone.
What wouldn't bring a penny in this wilderness,
go try to find its equal
in the rich towns of the world.
All's ego there,
so some are great and the rest little, unknown.
But where there's wisdom,
look—all are small, the unequal equal,
all a company of friends,
their eyes' light making anywhere a heaven."

I said,
"This is true, oh beautiful!
On your stem,
when under the wild beating of the hail,
you dance.
Remain in my heart
the only poem,
and purify it with your grace."

I lingered there till morning.
Then some Brahman broke
the bent branch of the vine.
"I go," the wild jasmine said,
"offering my life at the feet of the Beloved."
Silent, the morning wind
watched and passed on.

(1937)

2. Before the Revolution

Cloud Music

The wind drifts above the sea—
sorrow's shadow on a fitful joy;
wet magic of the ruthless storm
drenches the scorched heart of the world.
Here is your ship of war,
laden with aspirations,
rousing with the deep rolls of its wardrums
the seed slumbering in the earth's womb.
With hopes of new life they lift
their heads, they stare,
oh storm clouds!
Again and again
the thunder rumbles,
the rain pours down,
the heart of the world pounds
to the wild war-cries of the tempest.
Rising from sleep like a host of heroes,
their bodies pierced and wounded by the lightning flashes,
the mountain peaks
still struggle up to strike the sky.
The smallest plants
bear their little burden
smiling,
spread out in endless green,
shaking, quaking,
spilling flowers.
waving greetings,
calling you.
Only the small
can take a splendor from the storm.

Palaces are palaces no longer
but the dwelling-places of terror—
Over the mud only

will the water always pour and flow,*
spill always off the little blossoming lotus.**
So even miserable, diseased,
the fragile body of the child
will merely laugh.
While with his useless treasure,
his desperate pleasure,***
even in the arms of his beloved,
the rich man shivers,
clouds, frightened by your thunderbolts,
and hides his terrified face.

His arms shriveled, his body scrawny,
the anguished peasant calls to you,
you heroes of the storm-clouds.
They've sucked his juices dry,
he stands mere bones,
oh life-redeeming storm.

(1920)

Beggar

He comes along
grieving
down the road,
his heart in two pieces,
his belly and his back in one,
leaning on his stick as he walks,
with his old tattered bag gaping
for a handful of grain to kill his hunger.
Grieving he comes down the road
with his heart in two pieces.
Two children with him,
their hands stretched out always,
left hand rubbing the stomach as they walk,
right hand reaching out for a pitying glance.
When their lips shrivel up from starving
what recompense
from the generous Lord of destinies?
Well, they can drink their tears.
Sometimes they stand in the road
licking up the left-overs from a leaf-dish
and the dogs come hustling and snapping
to snatch it away from them.
Only wait—there's nectar in my heart—
I'll pour it out for you,
and you can be heroes
like Abhimanyu*
when I draw your sorrows
into my own heart.

(1921)

Breaking Stones

A woman breaking stones—
on a road in Allahabad I saw her
breaking stones.

No shade
from the tree under which she sat.
Her body black, her young breasts
bound tight in the *choli*;
eyes lowered,
mind turned to her lover
and acts of love.
The heavy hammer in her hand
struck time and time again.
Across the road long rows of trees
and high-walled mansions.
It was the hottest season,
the sun glaring,
and the scorching wind rose,
burning the earth like cotton,
with the air full of dust and sparks.
    It was noon by now,
    and she still breaking stones.
While I watched she saw me,
looked at me once,
then at the house, then at her ragged clothes.
Seeing no one else was there
she stared at me with the eyes
of one who doesn't cry
even when they beat her.
As from a tuned sitar
I heard a strain of music then
I'd never heard before.
After a moment she shuddered,
beautiful,

while the sweat trickled down her forehead,
then once more gave herself to her work
as though to say,
"I'm a woman
breaking stones."

(1935)

Giving

The early-risen sun
revels in the young bosom of the spring,
kissed, laughing, pliant, tender,
the rays like flickering girls, the lips
of the sprouting leaves red with the honey
of youth, the obliging bees in flight
from one opened bud to another
thrilling with new hope, new feeling,
the swarms in woods and gardens
sweetly buzzing in their bliss.
The cassias gold-garlanded,
the red-clad mirthful flame-of-the-forest,
the jasmine petals strewn as for
a ritual offering, and *mallika*
bursting into blossom;
the clustering *madhumadhavi*
lets droop its blooms as though in shame;
the lotus, opened for the first time, pure,
to stare upon the glorious mystery.
The breezes float their fragrance
along with echoed tales of lovers.
Capricious, slender as a dancer's waist,
twisting in her desire: the Gomti's stream.

Returning from a stroll this morning
I lingered on the bridge, thinking:
unalterable law of the world—
as you do so shall you be rewarded
by bountiful Nature herself—
there's nothing new to be said about this.
Beauty, song, the colors, scent,
speech and all the range of feelings,
and whatever higher joys may be:
these are the gifts of nature. Unsought

or labored-for they fall
to everybody's lot. And the best
of all (thanks be to God) is man's
high place as chief of all creation.

Then on the bridge I saw monkeys
beyond the counting crowded together.
And on the other side a man,
black-bodied, skeletal, half-dead—
misery given a human form—
staring unwaveringly in hope of alms,
throat shrunk, breath hoarse
merely to live a painful burden.
What curse had he brought on himself?
what sin committed to incur such grief?—
such questions come up often
in these streets and never get an answer.
The highest mercy—and all one could do—
was to give him a pice.

Leaning over I saw below
one of our glorious Brahmans
at his bath, pouring water
in the ritual offering to Shiva.
Taking his bag crammed with rice,
sesame and herbs he came back up.
The monkeys in a flash trooped around him.

This twice-born Brahman, devotee of Rama,
also worshipped Shiva with high hopes
the twelve months of the year. He was
my neighbor: always deep in the Ramayana
and muttering the holy name Narayana
and faithful in his daily ritual bath.
When suffering some minor grief
he'd join his hands*
and tell it to the monkeys.
From his capacious bag he took
some little cakes and flung them toward
the monkeys' outstretched hands.

He didn't so much as glance
where that other beggar sat
but screeched, "Out of the way,
you devil!" I said, "Well done,
you best of all creation."

(1935)

Blood Holi

(*Holi* is a rowdy spring festival, celebrated with bonfires, dancing and special songs, and throwing colored powders and squirting colored water. Nirala wrote this poem to honor the patriotism of the students who took part in the violent agitations of 1946.)

Boys and girls made life the game.
    They played Holi with their blood.
Among the people winning fame,
    they played Holi with their blood.

Bright as blossoms of the flame
    of the forest tree, bewitching as
crimson: lotus come to life—
    they played Holi with their blood.

How the red sprouts have started up,
    how the bonfires hurl their flames!
Singing the difficult songs of spring
    they played Holi with their blood.

Again the nights of song, again
    the brightening of the morning ray,
and flowers offered by every hand—
    they played Holi with their blood.

Enter a gaudy spring, clustered
    mango and lichi bloom.
the scent of jackfruit in the air—
    they played Holi with their blood.

The ebony trees put out their flags
    the cassias are hung with garlands;
scarlet flowers and red lips smiling—
    they played Holi with their blood.

(1946)

Love Song

I'm a Brahman's son
And I love her.

She belongs to the Kahars*
And at the first crack of light
She brings the water-jugs to my house,
And I'm dying for her.

She's black as a cuckoo, oh,
Her walk straight and steady,
And not yet married. My heart
Bursts with wanting her.

She comes every day and wakes us all
But I'm the only one who understands her game.
She takes away the big water jug
And I bide my time.

(1946)

from *Mushroom*

Outside the garden lay the huts;
from far off they looked sunk in the earth.
Filthy spot, the water stagnant
in the stinking drains. Its glory—
creeping vermin, scattered bones,
heaps of gristle and feathers,
chickens here, egg-shells there,
manure steaming in the sun.
Carried by the wind all kinds of stenches
spread everywhere.
Here lived the navab's servants,
most primitive of earth's creatures—
cooks, stewards and porters,
guards, grooms, waterboys, stable hands,
palanquin-bearers from round about,
barbers, washermen, potters, oil and betel men,
attendants for elephants and camels and carts:
a fine assemblage of Hindus and Muslims!
Their destinies were bound by one
same string, controlling all
the ups and downs of their existence.
Children, women, old men and youths
lived in this slum. Some gardeners too
had settled among them, for their bellies' sake,
and laughed and wept along with them.

(1942)

Have mercy Lord
on all
down-trampled people,
to all
poor wretches grant
the power of your
protection.

Mind and body fill
with clean love,
faces make
mild and kind,
on honest eyes
pour down
the dawning ray.

Let no head
before the mighty
bow.
The fitful heart
make constant,
and carry it
on the endless current
of its devotion
beyond
this life.*

(1939)

3. In the Forest of Panchvati

"*Panchvaṭi-prasang*" (literally, the Panchvati affair), the most ambitious of Nirala's early poems, is cast in the form of five dramatic fragments in unrhymed free verse. It is of particular interest in showing both how Nirala approached an episode from the epics and the degree to which he had absorbed ideas from Vedanta and the teachings of Sri Ramakrishna and Vivekananda. The subject of the poem is taken from the third book, "The Forest," of the Valmiki Ramayana, though certain details—notably Rama's expounding of the philosophy of non-dualism—have an antecedent in Tulsi's sixteenth-century vernacular version of the epic. In both Valmiki and Tulsi the episode occupies only a few lines, although it is the cause of all the later action of the epic—the abduction of Sita and the war with Ravana. Rama, his wife, Sita, and his brother Lakshmana are in exile in the forest of Panchvati, an exile that has taken on the characteristics of a pastoral idyll, when Shurpanakha, the sister of Ravana, demon king of Lanka, intrudes to shatter the Arcadian calm. For an understanding of the poem it is important to remember that Shurpanakha is not human, though she can assume human form, but an ogress, monstrously and bestially lustful and vain, and is clearly recognized as such by Rama.

The poem's vocabulary presents particular difficulties for the translator because of its exploitation of a seemingly inexhaustible supply of Sanskrit synonyms for certain adjectives and nouns (e.g., *beautiful* and *lotus*), which strains the resources of English, and the highly specialized philosophical terms used by Rama in his teaching. Nirala, however, characteristically does not scorn humbler Hindustani words in the speeches of both Lakshmana and Shurpanakha.

I

Sita

The memory of that day comes to me now,
beloved!
the day when in our flower-garden,
king of flowers!
beneath the rays of the young sun
the blue lotus, newly opened, laughed,
and you, bewitching-eyed, with Lakshmana
strolled contentedly.
But is not this scene, Lord, still lovelier than that?
That bower of vines was charming there,
but still more beautiful the cool roof
of jasmine spread atop that tree.
For now it seems to me, there I was a slave,
while here I play the game of freedom,
and you are with me.
Where else could I find greater ease?
Where else could I sit and watch
the quick-dancing feet of heavenly nymphs
on the flashing waves of the restless stream?
Where else could I hear
such birds trilling in the mild breeze
or the sweet singing of the Gandharvas*
within the rustling leaves?
Where else could I drink the sweet words from my beloved's mouth?
Or where else find
the clean radiance of insight, knowledge and devotion
except in a forest hermitage?

Rama

Within the little limits of a mean house
vile feelings are locked in—
this is the truth, beloved—
while the ocean of love spills over,
inexhaustible, on the earth.
The beating of love's mighty waves
shatters the mean frame,

scattering like straws
all the trivial desires of the worldly.
The ocean of love resounds with laughter
when it sees the entreaty
in the eyes of the terrified coward
standing silent on the shore,
hands joined, but steeped in illusions,
fearing to drown in that deep sea,
troubled by the hope of surviving,
which makes his whole body shrivel
as he remembers the fearful submarine blaze of passion—
and he turns his back on it.
Only one, beloved, with a body celestial
dares leap in—and he finds the nectar of love,
drinking which he becomes immortal.
And truly I find it too in sages,
a matchless love such as until today
I've never found before.
And more than any passion-blighted
palace pleasure garden
is this forest
pleasing to me.

Sita

Not for a moment was Lady Anasuya* wrong:
when just before setting out
I touched her feet with my forehead
she raised me up affectionately—
oh that gentle touch!—
and said, "Thou knowest, Sita,
the virtues of a faithful wife—
still let me speak to thee of them."
And all those qualities of wifeliness
respectfully she explained to me,
embracing me—how loving, oh,
how guileless and how selfless—
not for an instant do I forget it.

(Enter Lakshmana)

Lakshmana

Sir, some time ago, I brought
fragrant garlands of wood-apple
to our hut for the ceremony.

Rama

Yes, Lal,* we come.

Sita

And bring me Malti blossoms, Lal,
I myself will string them together
and offer them
at the dear and lovely feet
of my beloved husband.

(Exit Lakshmana)

How understanding he is!
Except to serve he's capable of nothing.
When he approaches he bows his head,
looks only at your feet,
and says, so like a child,
"Mother, what's your command?"

Rama

He has assumed all the virtues of his mother, Sumitra—
like her he's eager to serve, self-sacrificing,
like her simple, clean-hearted and luminous.
As Mother Sumitra pounced like lightning on any imperfection,
just so Lakhanlal* springs like lightning on the foe.
Did you not see his wrath in the fray with Parashurama?**
or at the time we set out for the forest?
Or when Bharat came up the mountain of Chitrakut?***
But you alone know how great
is his devotion to me.

II

Lakshmana

Service is the one recourse of life
and indeed the very precept of Mother Sita,
for whose love alone I garner flowers and leaves.
Apart from that I know nothing
nor have I even the desire to know.
My greatest strength is the very dust of her feet,
and her satisfaction, for me, equals the eight perfections,
and her affectionate words my highest joy.
Fortunate I am—
she for whose glance myriads of Shivas and Vishnus and Brahmas,
millions of suns, moons, stars and constellations,
of Indras, gods and demons,
universes of sentient and nonsentient beings
are born and bred and finally destroyed,
she who shines radiant in the very roots of all the Universes
as the primal shaping power,
by whose strength existence itself is in the strong—
she is my mother.
She, singing whose virtues men cross the ocean of being,
of whose reality alone is seen the firm impress
even in the "Om" of every charm and spell—
she is my mother.
She who has no equal
for her woman's greatness, her wife's devotion so profound,
she is my mother.
As a tangle of weeds afloat on the watery current,
homeless, aimless, without a will,
but—with the Lord's loving impulse in it—
finds at the end a sheltering heart vaster than the sea,
and so is freed,
so I too, renouncing the desire for pleasures,
home, riches and family,
I flow in the honeyed sea-wake of my Mother's feet.
I know not liberation, but devotion alone,
and it is enough.
If I but be the merest atom on her sweet lip,

that is the supreme bliss;
or if I could become a chakora* and go on drinking
the lily's night perfume rained in nectar from such a Moon—
for me what more contentment could there be?
No doubt of this:
it's an ill to be made happy,
to find one's happiness is far better.
When the pure drops of Mansarovar**
gathered by the sun's rays
take on their subtlest form, a form unmanifest,
they disappear for a time in the blue sphere of the sky,
singing an unheard melody—
they only know how great the bliss they find!
But meantime it is plain,
when they take on their cloudy shape,
signaling their advance,
then begins their youthful stage;
they change—how playfully! the colors
on the mountain peak, in the pathways of the welkin,
they dance, they mime, they shout and carol—
when the soft south wind kisses the cloud's tender cheek,
the heart fills with happiness,
and the bosom of Mansarovar is sprinkled with the drops,
breathing up watery sighs, remembering the past,
and when they see this wonder the multitude of blooming lotus,
tenderly smiling,
fling out a necklace of pearls.
For all of which I always hearken to the Supreme God:
"Oh Lord, folk call you the Wishing Tree
that grants the wish of every heart.
If you are content with me, oh Lord,
then this one boon I crave—
let me be sacrificed, utterly,
spirit and body,
for the satisfaction of the Mother;
let me know how to cut myself apart
from all trivial longings;
if any desire remain,
let it be for devotion."

It's late, I'll go now
and gather flowers.

III

Shurpanakha

When gods and Titans together
churned up the sea they took from it the fourteen jewels;
and I have heard,
two women, Rambhaa and Ramaa, came from that churning too,
said by all to be most beautiful.
And yet it seems to me
the Creator, squeezing out
the full portion of all the beauty in the Universe,
has filled this body with it—
with love—
else with his trembling fingers
the architect of this old scheme of things
had reduced all his artist's skill to dust.
And this is true as well:
no woman fairer has ever been conceived;
I'm a queen,
Nature my handmaiden:
when it sees my form
all the garnered loveliness of Nature humbly bows its head;
the woodland vines, wind-jostled,
all incline, lower their eyes,
as though hiding their faces at the sight
of this unparalleled beauty of mine.
Could even the Godavari stream,
reflecting the blue sky, the lightning and the stars,
and rushing swift as a girl to her lover,
be compared to these woven tresses,
laced with flowers, yet unbound?
Never!
Startled as a little girl would be
the imagination of poets
confronting my brows
whence shoot the bewitching arrows of primal sex,

in turn spell-casting, subjugating, mind-ravishing.
Overcome are all eyes that see those eyes,
for into them the Creator has poured
intoxication enough to make the whole world drunk.
The wondrous nose, fish-hook shaped to catch the god of love,*
these round cheeks, pink and soft as flowers,
the charming chin, flashing its laugh like lightning,
the mouth's sphere, with its far-reaching flower-fragrance,
that delights all the quarters with its scattered pollen
and entices the darling bees.
Regard this dove's throat,
the arms like lianas, the lotus hands,
the breasts swelling and erect, the narrow waist,
the capacious buttocks and the delicate feet,
the gait so graceful—
destroying the serenity of sages and ascetics:
truly a wondrous matter for gods and voluptuaries.
The greatest heroes fall at my feet,
like beggars craving my favors,
and folding their hands they say, "Fair one, be merciful now!"
But I, superb in triumph,
casting a scornful glance
on the vanquished heroes at my feet,
turn away my radiant world-conquering face.
What wonder in that?
Not long ago this glorious brightness was not here,
Nature cruel and violent stifled the very breath of life,
all places like a desert waste
threw up dust and scorched the body,
and helped by the fierce sun
cruelly tormented every wayfarer.
But today, what a transformation!
The hands of Nature, guilty no doubt of countless killings,
now serve, opening the portals of the heart,
eagerly bearing sweet fruit and cool water.
Hey dey! new animation finds its way into brute matter.
I feel an urge,
intoxicated now with love,
to sing strange songs with my attendant buds,

to play games with the flowers,
festooning myself with blossoms
and twining them in garlands around my throat.

(Decks herself with flowers.)

But what cottage is that?
Has some holy sage come?
I'll draw closer and find out
who's come to waste his life so stupidly here.

IV

Lakshmana

What do they mean by the end of the world?

Rama

The dissolution of mind, wisdom and ego is the end of the world.

Lakshamana

Tell me, Lord, how is that the end of the world?

Rama

Between the individual and the all there's no distinction—
distinctions are begotten by error,
which we call illusion.*

Not one man, brother, is ever deceived
by that light, through whose power
you see, resplendent, this solar universe entire.

The one form penetrates the individual and the All,
and is the source of bliss and understanding.
When curiosity stirs in the brain of the curious man,
when there's a longing to escape from error,
when consciousness gives warning: leave off your playing!
then a man's soul awakens
and he goes to dwell with sages and learn a discipline.**

No longer coarse, he becomes subtle and more than subtle;
when he begins to struggle with mind, widsom and ego
in the battle every day his strength increases two-fold.

Gradually he discerns
inside his very self
sun moon planets stars
and countless whirling universes.

Then he sees clearly
the World-soul within the ego,
and knows with certainty
that the individual is not to be distinguished from the All;
he sees, there is one cause and working
of creation, existence and dissolution,
and his desire is for skill in the fashioning,
the fostering and the dissolution.

So brother these all are qualities of Nature.
And true it is, then Nature gives him all its power—
and with the eight perfections
he becomes all-powerful,
and when he gives it up,
when he crosses the frontier of subject-and-object,
he mounts up to the seventh heaven—
even then is the world come to its end
and he takes on the ultimate form
of truth, spirit and bliss.

Lakshmana

Then how is the world created anew?

Rama

Those who through desire take body in this world,
their souls depart and come again
and their desire creates ever new creations.

For them, see, Lal,
all's useless here.

He who has become free
returns no more.

The endless series of myriad creations,
with them Nature sports for all eternity.

Well, these are other matters—
you asked about the dissolution of the solar universe.
Hear, brother,
just as the individual assumes one minute form,
just so the All
has its subtle state.
So all the seeds of Nature
are contained in the ether.
And it is also true that then
Nature's three basic strands* become identical.

Sita

These concepts are most perplexing, Lord—
tell us of the path of devotion!

Rama

The paths of devotion, action and knowledge are all the same
even though they appear different to the great authorities.

There's only One, no second's there at all.
The sense of Two is the only error.
And all the same, beloved,
from the very heart of error
we must rise and pass beyond it.

The sages first considered
the restlessness of men's minds.
Therefore they filled with devotion
those who had held to dualism.
To those thirsting for love
they taught the loving service of the people,
than which there is naught purer.
Through service the spirit is purified.

In the cleansed soul the seed of love springs up.

If the mind be not immaculate
then love is wasted
and draws men into bestiality.

Sita

Behold, Lord, a woman comes.

Rama

Sit now and let her approach.

V

Shurpanakha   (aside)

There are three of them here,
one more beautiful than the other.
The woman with them too
is fair and graceful—
but surely not more than myself.

           (Smiles a little, observing the garland on her breast.)

These handsome men, it's clear,
have never been ascetics;
those supple limbs have never endured austerities;
they must be princes
or else celestial heroes taking the forms of men
to wander in the forest.
The luster of the dark-blue lotus*
ravishes with ease
the love garnered in the heart—
the hidden riches of women.
I should like to spend this day in dalliance
on the lake's blue water,
drinking love's lotus nectar,
blooming, laughing, like the fortunate lily,
and sipping honey from the lips of the dark God.

           (Approaching Rama)

Oh beautiful!
your unequaled comeliness
has quite bewitched me.
As I am beautiful,
so you alone are worthy of me.
This will of mine insists
that you fulfill my wish.
Do not leave unanswered, man,
the urgent desire of a woman aroused!
Come you with me
to my forest, lover,
and I'll set you on a heavenly throne!
There's nothing will be denied you,
you'll taste divine delights, you best of men!
You shall be king over all in heaven
and I your queen.
Seated beneath the tree of Paradise you'll hearken to
the sweet-voiced Sirens' ambrosial morning song.
And when this jasmine bends quivering from its weight of bees—

Rama

Fair one, I'm married,
behold my wife.
But go to him,
a youth unmarried and handsome too.

Lakshmana

Fair one, I am his slave
and he the king of Koshala.
One wife? why, he can marry many times if he wishes,
but I'm his servant,
and hope of my pleasuring you
is wishing for flowers from the sky.

Shurpanakha   (to Rama)

You alone are worthy of me.

Rama

But just look and see
how fair he is, bright as gold!

Shurpanakha (to Lakshmana)

In the mirror of my heart
love's reflection—
how glorious, how radiant—
behold it!

Lakshmana

Be off, vile woman!

Shurpanakha (to Rama)

Shame, thou wretch!
Imposter! Cheat!
You've scorned one who came to you
with passion
ready to offer you her living youth.
Seeing you guileless, charming, fair as the god of love,
I thought,
he surely is some amorist,
skilled in the sensual arts.
How could I know,
this was the dark hue not of love
but of poison?—
and spread a fearful venom?
What I took for a rose
turned out, alas, a scentless jungle blossom.
My error—a mirage,
like the thirsting roe's in the parched desert.
As you have cheated me
so will you enjoy the fruit of it forthwith.
So long as breath is in me
I'll lie in wait for you like the black she-cobra.
I'll make you weep too
as you have made me weep.

Rama
I've not yet made you weep,
but if that is your wish—

>   (Signaling Lakshmana.)

Lakshmana
Now weep to your heart's content.

>   (Cuts off her nose and ears.)

(ca. 1922)

4. On Love and Nature

To Love

While finite nature still lay in the trance
of Infinity you, beginningless,
were only darkness, until perverse creation
stirred by its own desire alone was set
once more in motion. Fruit of delusion, you
descended then into the world,
kindling the lightning's magic in the breast,
ever transforming mere sensation into
substance, as waters turn to mist, then clouds.
Attired in the brilliant raiment of desiring,
creation became temptation. Forms, locking
their arms around each other, surmised, "Now we
have found it!" But then alas, bodies trapped
in the small errors of their judgment, they
both understood: love it had never been
but the shadow of love.
                              Yet love shall always be
the unstrung chain of diamonds on every breast,
though tangling every soul entangled never,
but ever the sovereign power.

(1938)

The Juhī Bud

On a vine in the deserted wood
she slept, blissful in dreams of love,
pure tender slender girl—
the *juhī* bud—
eyes closed, chilly in the folded leaf.
A spring night. Her lover,
tormented by separation in a distant land,
was that wind they call
the southern sandal-mountain breeze.
He recalled their sweet reunions,
the midnight drenched in moonlight,
the lovely trembling body of the girl.
And then? That wind
crossed over grove lake river mountain wood
and vine-entangled jungles
to reach where he could dally
with the budding flower.
She slept—
for, tell me, how could she suspect
that her lover was at her side?
The hero kissed her cheek,
and she swayed, shivering from it,
but even now she did not waken
nor ask forgiveness for her fault.
The long curved sleepy eyes stayed shut
as though she swooned, intoxicated
from the wine of youthful longings—
who can say? Ruthless, her lover,
of a sudden cruel,
struck that tender body hard,
slapped her pale full cheeks.
The girl started up,
stared all about her, astonished,

and found her darling by her bed.
She smiled, gratified in her desire,
and blossomed in her lover's arms.

(1916?)

To a Waterfall

Restless little waterfall,
tumbling radiant from the mountain,
why do you play
with the deep dark of the forest,
what's your reward?
Are you so much in love with darkness?
God knows whether it's
a child's game, lacking all sense,
or the Buddha's serene indifference.
If you stumble on some
stupid envoy from your mountain home—
that is, trip on a stone—
you turn and pause an instant;
then, recognizing it for what it is
in its poor lifeless ignorance,
you dimple to a tolerant smile—
that's all—
you wink at its simplicity
and move on,
the while within its heart
your song resounds.

(1921)

Song

Lover, the night has wakened.
Her drowsy eyes, half-closed lotuses,
yearn for her young lover's sun-bright face.

The splendor of her loosened hair
floats over neck shoulders arms and breasts,
making her glance another sun
lurking behind the clouds,
its rays her bright limbs.
Outdone, the lightning flash
craves her forgiveness.

Covering her breast, she tosses her hair behind her,
stares all around her and walks with a swan's grace.
In her house she is
the victory garland of her husband's love:
unburdened of desire, a pearl
sewn with the thread of renunciation.*

(1927)

Done

(A village girl speaks to another)*

You didn't pick your fill of flowers,
my dear, and now the spring is gone.
Is it not cruel—the way
the heart's gladness is snatched away?

Helpless, I watched, eyes smiling, enchanted
and even as I watched, alas, I tired.
My feet weary, I stood in the road like one deceived;
from tormented blossoms a glorious fragrance drifted, saying:

"You didn't pick your fill of flowers,
my dear, and now the spring is gone.
Is it not cruel—the way
the heart's gladness is snatched away?"

I remember now
a certain day
when the wind was still
and the sky dreary.
The sullen sun had covered up his face,
on the heart's lotus the bleak ray, and the whole forest
sad—as I stood I saw the splendor. And he,
taking this hand of mine in his, said:
"There'll be a day
When I won't be.
Is it not cruel—the way
the heart's gladness is snatched away?"

(1921)

Because, my dear, I love him, does he also love me?
I flow toward the unknown, and the whole world flows with me.

My feet did not stop on the stairs
though I saw Death in wait for me.
I have broken through the walls of my house,
    deserted my home and family.

I don't know: did I cut myself loose, was I swept away?
Did I draw him to me or was I drawn?
I remember no longer what I did
    nor whether I won or lost.

When I opened my eyes I was floating still,
rising and falling on the tides of my affection,
and nourished again and again with bliss
    I adorned myself for love.

I have garnered all the blossoms of my deeds,
and in the desert, counting my lover's qualities,
skilfully made of them—hear me!—a garland
    and set it on him.

(ca. 1928)

To the Flower by the Wayside

Pathetic as a beggar's wallet,
downcast blossom! Tell me why
you lie flung in the dust,
looking a silent tragedy,
poignant as rāg Desh*—
what do you say
when you spy some traveler passing by?
"The tree, assaulted by the gusting wind,
survived; but alas it bent too far,
ripping away the helpless vine,
and the tempest carried me away—
whence my calamity."
Not so? Then tell me what.
"At the hour of sacrifice to Shiva and Uma
no one has ever proffered you on the altar,
his body marked with holy sandal paste
and his selfishness hid in his heart.
Though offering your all,
scent color beauty,
you wither in a day;
and seeing you a trifle wilted,
he tosses you on the ground—
that brute with a stone for his heart."
Nor this? Then why so sad,
why drift and moon about this way?
What do you say?
"That night has passed:
the passionate meeting of two lovers—
sweet spectacle of fulfilment—
when the two devotees were lost
in the rites of love,
and used me alone in the fair devising of their worship,
made me privy to their dalliance,
and I alone played the priest—

when the tender hand met the lotus hand
through me alone did they perfect their ritual.
I was the single link in the bond of love;
I was the metaphor and meter both
of the music that they made! "*

(before 1930)

Recognized

I recognized you,
this time I recognized you,
blooming in that garden,
swaying as you kissed
the golden cheek of Usha,*
playful and winsome,
naively making plain
your precious honeyed meaning.
Dressed for a holiday you greeted all alike,
your veils drawn back
to show your very nature's countenance
for your devotees' delight.
How could that ruthless gardener understand
your generous heart?—
he a mere rustic lout!

Cursed with his selfishness
he came blundering along.
For a paltry coin he ended that joyous life
forever, broke it off the moment your stem
inclined to him.
And with the heart in him harder than a stone
he went away,
that murderous gardener.

(before 1930)

First Dawn

There came to me just now
a shivering breeze, like a perplexed kiss;
it shook the edges of the troubled sky,
stirred a first sweet twinge of shame;
unsteady red on the lips of the goddess of Dawn,
poured unfamiliar feelings into the eyes
of a girl in love, a knowledge
of the rising of the red, youthful sun,
a fragrance spilling out intoxication;
gently striking the window
of a dream-entangled adolescence,
seizing the thread of self-command
and pulling it toward itself,
like the gathering rhythm of the unborn stream
before it gushes in a rapture
from the mountain's secret places.
I woke and opened my door,
found on my face the authority of the rays.

(before 1930)

Paradise

When we shut our eyes what will they give us?
   sight of the eternal lover?
   the spell of the brimming cup
      for endless thrilling lives?
   battle without dying?
   dust of the Lord's holy feet?
   the kiss like lightning
      piercing through the clouds?
   or—though unresisted blessed
   with the charm of real resistance—
      the serene embrace?

(before 1930)

A Solution

"Will not the golden blossoms
    wither in the winds of Time?
and from the eyes will not
    the splendor of youth decline?"

And still my joy-giving youth
    will every instant fill
the empty heart of all
    old songs, the ever youthful
source of all creation.

Since after all we shall remain
    deluded sinners,
kissing the atoms of darkness,
why shouldn't youth's delusive splendor
    remain
after all the same?

(before 1930)

Eyes

Are they wicked?—
ecstatic blue-lotus eyes!—
or distraught, like little fish in shallow water?
or pathetic, as though waiting for someone
as the nights pass by?
or straying like restless travelers?
They say:
"We're ascetics,
we can bear all sorrows.
We take the days of heat, of cold, of rains.
We flow with the waves of the waters of time.
We're silent, but we understand
what secrets lie hidden in growth and decay,
in the rapturous music of the flute
that praises the Divine. But all the same
It fills our meditation.
How many troubled minds we've known,
how many hearts we've shaken and brought to bloom,
in what fires of love's affliction we have burned,
what sorrows of those lovers borne!"
Why are they silent for me alone?
Are they tender blossoms, traveler?
What are they?

(before 1930)

Misunderstanding

Lover, you couldn't understand—
when overcome your eyes looked away,
when, my heart full of elation,
my breast trembled
and you saw the trembling
of my jasmine garland
—the beauty!

(1937)

Song

Shedding its last rays the sun
    goes down to its other world.
With weary steps folk come home,
    each man to his own door.
Down the skyways slow descending
    the darkening evening
sets the tender burden
    of her feet upon the earth.
Quietly the breeze pours out,
    the flower of the woodvine opens,
its petals shaping to folded palms
    offering reverence.
The beloved rises, arrayed in beauty,
    her eyes inclined downward,
and begins the ceremony of the lamps
    lighting up the house.

(1934)

Consoled

Life
a long time now
has burned

in the hot sun,
earth parched,
parched tree,
the watering ditch
parched,
bees' buzz
ceased,
dust-dim
the groves,
but on the sky's breast,
friend,
a garland of blue clouds.

(1937)

Clear Skies

After many days, clear skies,
the sun ablaze, the world content.

Horizons open, trees shine forth.
Sheep and buffalo are set to graze.
Children squabble and play and tease,
and daughters make their houses bright.

From village to village people wander,
some to market, some to sit
and chat beneath the banyan trees,
while sturdy lads strip down to wrestle.

Girls crowd together at the well,
today not caring if water splashes
on their skirts. How the gossip flies
as they stand there and shoot
the well-aimed arrows of their eyes!

(1938)

5. Remembering Saroj

(Written after the death of the poet's daughter, Saroj. The name means lotus; throughout the poem the many synonyms for lotus and the flower's many conventional epithets in Sanskrit and Hindi are called upon to reinforce and lend a poignant resonance to this evocation of Saroj's life and her significance for Nirala.)

Scarcely nineteen you took one step and crossed
the whole of life, my daughter, closed your young
eyes to your father, and said farewell to living.
My song, you shed this individual self
and entered forever freedom beyond the changing.
You had lived out your eighteen years fulfilled
and pure when your swift feet mounted the ship
of death, as though to say, "Father, I choose
the full light. This isn't dying but only
the lotus-brightening, a crossing over."

Being a poet I had some understanding
so I might catch the speech of silent lips.
I'd made my offerings day and night to luminous
Sarasvati. Living poem of mine,
when you abandoned me on earth, pierced
by every arrow, did you go to heaven
thinking, When my father makes the journey
he'll find the going hard, and then I'll help
him through the darkness? So spoke your easy going,
it had no other meaning when you left us
under the bleak sky of the first day
of the bright half of the rainy month.

Daughter, I was a worthless father, did
nothing for you. Although I knew some ways
of earning, I would always let them slip
away, knowing as I well knew the wrongs
attending the path to wealth. I always lost
the struggle for success. And so, my dear,
I couldn't dress you in silk or even give you
enough to eat. But I could never snatch
the poor man's bread or bear to see him weep.
In my tears I always saw reflected
only my own face and my own heart.

Humbly I'd think, time and time again:
my work is a gift of love to Hindi—not
defeat but a victory garland, an offering
superhuman. There were other ways

but I proved myself only with my skill
and sacrifice to literary art,
leaving for others mere acquisition,
and devoted all my powers to prose and verse.

Others who watched were quick to laugh, but watch
the battle was all they did. The swift arrows
rained on me, wounding me times innumerable.
Throughout the grueling fight I did not flinch
beneath those arrows, but caught in art the music
of struggle, fruit of the cruel battlefield.
The beauty of it will bear still more fruit,
awakening a sun in every life.

Just look—taking her artist's brush
what colors would Sarasvati pour out,
what charm desired by me reflect, and with
her love what real fulfilment grant my art?

And so, unskilled at earning, I denied
you what was due. When once you stayed some days
with me, bowing your head with dignity,
my daughter, even in your father's house,
before leaving that sorry yard your eyes
let go the tears of your suppressed desires,
and you sighed such a little sigh for all
the longings buried in your heart.
I understood, and I looked on, wondering
what I could do to help, and I did nothing.

At fifteen months we saw how quick you were
in understanding; your mother kissed and kissed you,
as with your life you gave new life to her.
Her story ended, and she left us. Then I
gave you into her mother's keeping. There
existence was all pleasure, night and day.
Though sometimes put out by your brother's teasing
you wept, tears glistening in your lotus eyes,
and understanding he would coax you, take
you walking down along the Ganges banks.

Your tear-washed face shining with laugher
you'd watch the vast reaches of bright waves.

In those days too I was engrossed—in vain—
in being a poet, writing ceaselessly
verse known as "free"; but the flock of editors,
no wise impressed, skimmed through it all and sent it back
with a line or two in answer. Then I'd go
to sit for a long while out in the yard,
staring at the sky, and pondering the virtues
of editors. And following my custom,
I'd pinch the grass around me, toss it away
at random, working out my feelings on it.

One morning, I remember, for the first time
the sunlight fell full on you, showed your beauty—
you playing like a restless spirit. I'd come,
after two years away, to Sasu's house*
eager to see you with my own eyes.
I sat outside on a cane stool by the gate,
holding in my hand my horoscope
with the long long tale of my life. I read
in it of two auspicious marriages,
and I laughed, in my heart a great desire
to wipe out this scribbling about my fate;
I looked to the future unafraid.

Before this too my own people had said
affectionately, "Life would be happy
if you could find some educated and
attractive girl." Many offers were broached.
Politely I rejected them. To all who came,
entreaty in their eyes, intent on my
acceptance, I would say, unhesitating,
"I'm *mangali*"**—hearing which they turned away.
Once there were complications, a proposal
in no way easy to reject; I felt
the full charm of those eyes, and Sasu told me,
"My dear, they're fine important people; the girl
has her degree. They said, 'He's twenty-six,

high time he was a bridegroom, and the girl
is just eighteen.' And they folded their hands and pleaded:
'He's a true gentleman, a poet, a regular sage,
and he has a good name, and our own girl
is educated, beautiful. It's fitting
for you to tell him all these things. He'd be
a happy husband.' They'll be back tomorrow."
My look turned cold; before my eyes appeared
your image, blithe, laughing. I was myself
again, considered this marriage sensibly.
I picked up the horoscope and showed it to you.
"Here, take it," I said, giving it to you. "Play."
Then Sasu came back, fresh from her bath, hair down,
in her best clothes, smiling mysteriously
and talking of the inevitable subject:
what to expect tomorrow. Amused, I pointed
to those tattered remnants of the horoscope;
dismayed, she watched you sitting amidst the scraps.

As time went by you stepped beyond the realm
of childish games; the beauty of your age
rounded to fullness, an element of grace
settled on your sweetness, trembling, vibrant,
like Malkauns lightly sounded on a new vina.*
Awakening gradually from night-dreaming like a dawn
that rises on the rhythm of the morning hymn, and trembling
with the burden of your own light—so trembled the forest,
the morning skies; with each experiencing
of yours all bloomed,
sky earth tree bud and blossom.
That look of yours! streams inexhaustible
and bountiful rose gushing like waters
in a blue tumult, but—checked by the holy bonds
that limit the body—from your eyes
came only tears in gentle moderation.
And in your voice your mother's nuanced sweetness,
beloved music, sounded exuberantly**
the very notes of my elation. My darling,
a singer natural born, you were the music
for my verse made visible in loveliness—

I'd not dared hope for such a blessing during
this incarnation. Such music was never heard
before from one unschooled. But then, I knew
that when the cuckoo's child first nourished in
an alien nest has learned to fly her voice will sound
in some new forest, silent up till now.
To me you were all beauty manifest
as in your own heart woke the cherished poet;
there started up an unfamiliar wind
that moved to resonance all stored-up feelings
for tree bud blossom everything together
as it caressed your hair and fragile limbs.
You watched it all, your eyes unwavering,
and then I understood your life.

Looking at you one day Sasu said,
"It was our duty to bring her up, but now
it's time to give Saroj into the hands
of a good husband with an honorable name—this is
our holy obligation. Take her now
to your own house for a while and seek a groom
worthy of both of you. We'll gladly help
arrange her wedding."
                              Silently I listened,
reflected, said nothing, neither "no" nor "oh,"
and took you with me, my golden girl, like a beggar
hastening a costly treasure, bright as dawn,
into the darkness of his house. Cast down,
I thought, over and over again,
"These Kanyakubja Brahmans*—they burn down
their own houses, they bite the hand that feeds them.
Marrying Saroj to one of them could be
a source of grief, since poisoned fruit alone
grows on the poisoned tree. They'll prove a desert,
and marriage a mirage." But then I thought,
"It's right that I should travel the path traveled
by my forefathers—why should I not fulfill
the accepted ritual?" But I'd never feared to go
against established custom, and how could I
stomach the folly of all those absurd traditions?

I was not humble enough to violate,
for them, my natural feeling. Those Brahmans:
dirty and dry as Jamna sandbanks; glum
faces of eaters of borrowed food; like feet
blistered in painful leather shoes, oiled
and squeaking and foul-smelling—I'm not
so blind I can do homage to such feet,
or reverence people so devoid of worth.
To wed my Parvati to such a Shiva
is not at all what I desire. Then I
recalled, a while ago I'd met a boy
involved in literature, a Kanyakubja—
perhaps a sign of luck beyond the grasping.
He promised well, seemed worthy of our welcome,
and I made my resolve, my heart opening
with new affection. I wrote to him to come
at once, and the boy himself was overjoyed.
I told him, "I'm empty-handed now. I could
pledge my inheritance to the moneylenders
to make a match with some rich fellow—but such
is not my wish, nor am I such a fool
as to attempt to give a dowry. Why
at such a joyous time crave ostentation?
If you agree I'll break the custom,* dispense
with the usual astrological reckoning.
And if the priests refuse, then I'll perform
the ceremony myself. And understand,
all that I have belongs to her, my chaste,
my well-born girl."

        The priest did come, and friends,
my fellow writers with their kin, and saw
a wedding of a new kind. On you the splendor
was poured out with the pitcher's holy water.
You looked at me, and on your lips a smile
like lightning, yourself the image of your joy,
the music of your lover's silent love.
Your beauty opened on a sigh, your faith in him
possessed you; from your cast-down eyes the light
fell trembling on your lips. In you I saw
the courage, the first singing of my own spring,

that love without embodied form, the feeling
I'd poured out in my poems and once had sung
with my lost darling, filling my senses now
with passionate joy. Just such was Rati* taking
a human form, like heaven metamorphosed
into substantial earth.

The wedding ended. Of my own relations
not one was there, nor had they been invited.
No wedding music filled the house to keep
us all awake both day and night. But a silence
full of new life and love spread music everywhere.
I gave you then a mother's last instructions,
myself arranged for you the marriage bed,
and thought: she is Shakuntala! But here's
a different lesson and a different art.

You'd stayed a while with us at home; and then
secure and happy in your grandmother's lap,
loved by your aunt and uncle as the cloud
that gives the water loves the earth, sheltering
through your sorrow and joy, devoted all
to you. They were the vine on which you budded
and blossomed, nourished with love. And at the end
again you found a refuge in their house,
there closed your dying eyes.

Of me so long unlucky you
had been the one blessing. Deprived of you
two years later, life remains
one tale of woe: how can I tell it now
when I could not before? Let the lightning fall
on all my work, and if it be my fate,
I'll go on down this road, head bent, but perish
my works like lotuses blasted by the winter.
To you, daughter, I sacrifice the karma
of all past lives as offering to your spirit.**

(1935)

95

6. Evening Music

I'm Alone

I'm alone.
I see
the evening of my day draw near.

My hair is white and sparse,
my cheeks sunken,
my walk ever slower:
the festival is over.

I know I've crossed
the rivers and torrents I had to cross.
I laugh now as I see
there wasn't any boat.

(1940)

99

Don't see yourself as alien,
 don't call the alien your own.
Don't think dreams are imagination,
 don't call imagination dreams.

For the honor of the eye
 live with the eye of honor.
For austere meditation sit indeed,
 but don't call sitting meditation.

Hold together like the bubble,
 let go like the rose.
The eye beautiful from falling asleep
 don't call a closing of the eye.

(1942)

Don't tie the boat up here, friend!
The whole village would wonder, friend!

This is the very landing where
laughing she'd step into the stream to bathe.
My glance caught, she'd stare back,
and my legs would tremble, friend.

Her laugh said almost everything,
but she kept her feelings to herself.
Heard everyone and bore with everyone,
but gave them all the slip, friend!

(January 21, 1950)

What opens
will decline;
what flies high
will fall a good fall.

So the saying goes:
you're in a mess, wringing your hands;
then the unsplit gram, floating useless,
suddenly bursts and saves the soup.*

If the signal doesn't work
all is shadow, all's illusion.
But the smile that reaches the heart
brings fulfilment.

The curse that turned pride to fear
proved the blessing of my life.
With a sweet grave sound from the mountain's heart
the spring streams forth.

(January 24, 1950)

Dense darkness shrouds the earth,
the ship dips wildly in the storm.

The pilgrim is a captive in the temple,
the elephants rant in the wood,
the child without a reason cries,
for the provider no one provides.

The waters moil and whirl,
then fall back feebly lapping.
Mountains rise, then split the earth;
the night is a fatal spell.

Alive though stale and withered,
though empty, clinging to existence,
drinking up the purity of the heart:
such is this unprofitable journey.

(January 24, 1950)

Why have you forgotten me?
and cut not just the branches
but the root?

While the world turned hotter
drinking the sun's fierce rays
with the wind you smashed the tree that shaded me
down into the dust.

Broken the discipline of the flesh,
fruitless the ceremony of love,
the house at night without a lamp—
first you put out the fruit and then the flowers.

Not known: why you sprang into life,
why such a cruel wound was dealt,
why the pure body was defiled,
why you turned averse to growing.

(January 25, 1950)

Make all things natural:
fill me like a pitcher
with the essence.

You cheated every heart,
pillaged all treasure;
in such a pass, a curse
on youth, on life.
Your grace grant else
I'll not suffice.

The world's net's spread,
part and parcel illusion,
no road can be traced
in the spreading darkness;
black error pierce now
with your arrow.*

(February 6, 1950)

Whoever's spent
these days of sorrow
counting and counting
the minutes, the trifles,
has strung a necklace
of tears like pearls
and tossed it around
his lover's throat
to see the lovely face
serene and bright
in the night of sorrow.

(February 6, 1950)

The cuckoo speaks in every grove,
his notes shot through with rapture.

The dense new-leaving woods have trembled,
like ears the caves resound with joy;
the natural covering of the world draws taut,
veins and sinews test their power to feel.

Garnering in its rays the subtle stars
the bright live sun comes round its course of love.
Filled with drunken music sweetly humming
the bud sways with the bee.

(February 7, 1950)

At the touch of my lover's hand I woke.
So I had fallen asleep, unlucky girl.

The flowers of the weeping tree* have fallen,
the doorway fills with golden beams,
the birds' sweet babble by now has faded.
Marked with ashes the ascetic has set out.

Deep in their studies are all the children,
the master of the house is at his morning worship,
the mistress makes all ready for the bath,
and at the door the beggar's cry is heard.

(February 7, 1950)

Every thread was worn out
when I saw a brand new
dawn sewn tight again,
sweet music shook my heart,
I heard spring's drowsy buzzing—
but then oh my body
was already cold.

The path-way of the eyes
opened,
the bud's sweet fragrance
mingled,
what was held inside
was swindled,
from the body scent and color
faded.

Now the talking's stopped,
the heat's been cooled,
sin washed and ironed out,
and the ray
fallen on the noisy mouth.

(February 10, 1950)

Guide the ship
to the other shore.

Hands tired with rowing.
no one along with me,
my forehead sweating, and oh
between the two banks!

When I crossed the woods
my face drooped and wilted.
Come and make an ending
of my calamity.

The whirlpool's got the boat;
forgotten all evasions—
the river current, oh!
won't stop roaring.

(February 10, 1950)

With sweetest tones you called,
death coming in disguise.

West wind sowed the poison,
clouds drizzled down the wine,
in the tune the rataplan of death,
with ending spreading through the notes.

You sang the ceased rhythm in the feet,
in the breath reduction to emptiness,
in beauty unequal riches,
and in your shelter no protection.

(February 12, 1950)

Let me walk the straight path,
Let my life put out
only its own fruit.

High aspirations—crushed,
and the wounds have brought me low;
the bad fruits born of my own heat—
let them burst like blisters.

Where life's every minute's a worry—
what health, what wisdom there?
Let me bear my sickness as fruition
and be ground by the hand of my deserving.

(December 7, 1952)

Body broken, mind sick,
life an anguished forest.

Flesh dwindling minute by minute,
blasted the gorgeous dwelling,
the rain closing in,
downpour of the last day.
Hand doesn't move,
nobody's near—
up, the bowed head,
who moves all sinners,
give shelter!

(December 8, 1952)

A little boat,
a golden evening,
rays spread like lashes.
A girl
fair as Parvati
plays the vina;
towards the east the boat
goes drifting; a Rajput boy
gives the rhythm
with a steady clapping
of his hands.
The lad's a singer too,
and there are folk aplenty
sitting around to listen.
And both of them serene
while the boat
goes drifting,
gently rocking,
easing the heart.

(December 9, 1952)

Where man's no better than a horse or ox
how can the mind and body pair together?
Whatever fraud of self-control's invented,
whatever obstacle's made of the flesh,
the clever modern man considers it
a mere scourge for barbarous passion.
Belief having taken off from these parts,
when the dirt came out of learning
it festered and festered until it burst
like a boil in the rainy month.

(December 16, 1952)

Plowing done the team comes home,
yoke set over the bullocks' shoulders,
on the bar the upturned plow,
reins in hand the aging father,
and the mother, bundle steady on her head;
father goes to the village corral,
mother home, and the boys come running.

There are mangoes and roseapples,
some figs and unripe *gullu*;*
the boys go wild picking them out—
there are real ones on every tree.
Then the eldest son's wife
sets out the little sweet cakes
and gets Manni to cook them.

(December 16, 1952)

Flower garden
like
a fragrant sari.

    Bejeweled with blooms,
    rooted vines climbing,
    billowing west wind,
    flowing channels.

    Shall I say,
    a mist has spread?
    the garden flickers
    with dusky melons
    and beds of gourds.

(December 16, 1952)

Beneficent our honored Sharda*
has put on the Spring's fair garland.

Folk quit their sorrow, their eyes
Flock skyward with a thousand wings;
the cuckoos on the mango branches
sing your carols to the heavens.

Peacocks dance at break of dawn,
stealing pleasures under clouds of leaves.
The heart of the girl in love is freed from spells
and the jasmine hankers for blossoming and loving.

(February 2, 1954)

Fresh clouds cover the black sky,
spread over forests, mountains, gardens, faces,
      touching the mango-heavy orchards,
      pouring over the rice fields.
      A girl comes out, the pitcher in her hand,
      embracing the east wind like a lover;
      the water churns in the lotus pond,
      the ditches overflow,
      the drunken river rushes on;
      and the joy of swinging
      from a neem tree on the bank.

(August 15, 1955*)

Shining autumn fills the skies,
the lilies dance in every pond.
   At dawn shephali blossoms fall,
   poor bodies shamed by the sunbeams.
   Brooks and rivers dwindle now.
   In every house they change to warmer clothes.
The nights are turning quieter,
the sun's husbandry more fruitful.
In the villages the paddy reapers
gather before their houses to talk and laugh.
   The wagtails reappear, the ibis
   and the cranes are back, covering the trees.
   And the beauty ripples like a wave
   in the eyes of the girl with the lovely lashes.

(November 8, 1955)

The buds have come back to the jasmine,
the branches smile with bees.
 What lived without a drop of water
 suddenly grown rich sucks nectar.
 Pleasures course through every vein,
  waves spill gurgling out of the canals.
Songs of the rains and all twelve months
fly up and brighten the eastern wind.
 Men's fortunes are reversed,
and every leaf begins to breathe.
 Drawn by the mangoes' fragrance
 wandering folk come back home.
 Wreaths of flowers hang from every door
 and rivers overflow their banks.

        (July 28, 1958)

The poison of a life
infected with literature
has been exhausted.
In my inmost heart the lamp
of the divine command is lit.
One ray shows the road
through the dark, like
the pole star amid the constellations.
The ending of the play—a flowering
whether it bore fruit
or withered barren,
a holy sage's on a bed of leaves
or just some ordinary man's.
Bhishma
on the cruel bed of arrows
turns his gaze upwards.
The fiery heat has cooled,
the rains ended too;
at dawn filaments of dew
cover the autumn lotus.
The cold broken, spring mangoes
put out their scented blossoms.
My armies that reached the four horizons
are done with:
restrained and measured verse,
melody, style, essential feeling;
and from my hand
the sweetly rhythmed instruments
have dropped.
My work—a failure,
the struggles of every warrior
petered out,
the target missed.
My hide,
once tensed for a shield
has gone slack.
Another dawning,
another turning
and returning
of the heart.

(1961)

Afterword: The Poetry of Nirala

Pant to Nirala:

> Weak my human spirit, and the world
> unfathomable, uncrossable.

Nirala to Pant:

> The road I know I tell—
> burn in your heart with doubled fires;
> by so much as you burn away
> flesh and pride
> just so much will be the light you find.*

* Quoted from a quasi-humorous exchange of letters, dated respectively January 3 and January 6, 1931, before the poets' first meeting, published first in the journal *Hans* (January, 1931) and reprinted in *Git Gunj*. Pant's letter, in archaising couplets in Braj, provoked Nirala to answer in Bengali, "my first poem in this language," as he says. It is interesting as one of the few surviving examples of Nirala's Bengali verse, which tends in general to be, like this letter, light and epigrammatic and quite free of the influence of Tagore.

THE POETRY of the "Chhayavad" group and the later fiction of Premchand together represent the first, and thus far the finest, flowering of
the new literary Hindi, based on *khaṛī bolī* (the "straight" or "pure
speech") that became accepted as standard during the last half of the
nineteenth century and the first two decades of the twentieth. The
credit for the triumph of the *khaṛī bolī* phase of Hindi over Braj is
usually attributed to Pandit Mahavir Prasad Dwivedi, who devoted
himself energetically to the reform and propagation of *khaṛī bolī*, particularly from 1903 to 1920 when he was editor of the influential
journal *Sarasvatī*. But although he contributed greatly to the improve-
ment of Hindi style and diction and to the development of its literary
potential, it is also true that the so-called "Dwivedi-yug" saw the
creation of no masterpieces in the new idiom. None of the poets
published in *Sarasvatī* during Dwivedi's editorship commands much
more than historical interest now with the exception of Maithili
Sharan Gupta, whose great work, in any case, was not to appear
until the thirties.[1] It was the Chhayavadins who first fulfilled the prom-
ise of the Bharatendu and Dwivedi periods with the publication of
such volumes as Nirala's *Anāmikā* (first version 1922) and *Parimal*
(1930), Prasad's revised *Jharnā* (1927), Pant's *Pallav* (1928), and Mahadevi Verma's *Nihār* (1930).

Among the four remarkable poets who formed the nucleus of the
Chhayavad movement Suryakant Tripathi "Nirala" was easily the
most extraordinary figure. His eccentricities, his generosity, the power
of his personality and the bellicose spirit which led him into so many
notorious imbroglios (such as those with Gandhi and Nehru), all made
him noteworthy even in that most colorful of Indian literary eras. The
pen-name he chose, "Nirala"—the strange one—was no misnomer.
That he was also the finest of the Hindi poets of his time was not so
quickly recognized. During his lifetime recognition came to him much
more slowly than to Prasad and Pant, and the official imprimatur, in
the form of national awards, was never accorded at all. His work was
too startling in its originality, his language too difficult, his satire too
bitter, his break with the past too offensive to the orthodox, and the
depth of his feeling either too troubling or too far beyond the common ken to assure wide popularity. Even today, for all the lip-service
Nirala is likely to receive from university Hindi departments in India,
there is no critical, nor even a collected, edition of his poetry or prose,
and some of his most important works have been out of print for
several years.

The Chhayavad Movement

"*Chhāyā*" may be translated either as shadow or reflection. The word makes plain the movement's predilection for symbolism and mysticism. The writings of the Chhayavadins were in general highly subjective, their symbols often private or abstruse, and their main themes love, nature, and the yearning of the soul for the Infinite. Chhayavad represents a revolt against both Braj poetry (still faithful to the 250-year-old traditions of the "Riti" era) and the *kharī bolī* poetry of the Bharatendu and Dwivedi periods, which the *Hindī Sāhitya Kosh* succinctly terms "savorless, preachy, matter-of-fact and coarse."[2] What is most remarkable about the emergence of this introspective and romantic school is that it coincides with the political and social ferment of the twenties and thirties, the age portrayed so harshly and painfully in the mature novels of Premchand. Nirala was, in fact, the only one of the Chhayavadins whose poetry reflects a preoccupation with contemporary problems. Although Prasad shows his social awareness in his novels, his poetry is given over to highly personal lyrics, to reconstitutions of an ideal and remote past, or to the elaborate allegory of his masterpiece, *Kāmāyanī*, drawn from mythological sources. Pant, for his part, even when his poems portray village life and reflect occasionally his interest in Marxism, remains subjective, romantic and preoccupied with esthetics and metaphysics. Virtually all of Mahadevi's poetry is confined to elaborating the relationship with the divine lover. But Nirala, from the very beginning, with poems like "Cloud Music" (1920) and "Beggar" (1921), was dramatizing the predicament of the poor and calling for revolution at the same time that he was creating some of his most exquisite lyrics, poems like "The *Juhī* Bud" and "Evening as a Girl." This reminds us that Nirala has never been easy to classify, another way by which he has made critics uneasy.

Chhayavad was followed by various new schools, such as "Progressivism" and "Experimentalism," social or psychological in orientation but owing much to the liberating achievements of the Chhayavadins. Prasad died in 1937 at the age of 48. Mahadevi in the forties turned generally from poetry to the writing of criticism and prose sketches. Pant, ever immensely productive, was for a while preoccupied with social and historical themes, but his chief impulse has always been clearly romantic. Nirala, on the other hand, continued until his death in 1961 to experiment with new styles and forms, evolving astonishingly in technique and range of perception in a way that may justly be compared with the evolution found in the work of Yeats.

Nirala's Life

Suraj Kumar Tevari, later known as Suryakant Tripathi and from 1923 on as "Nirala," was born in 1899[3] in the village of Mahishadal, Midnapur District, Bengal, in a family of Kanyakubja Brahmans who had migrated from Gadhakola in the Kanauj region of the U. P. His father was an officer in the court of the Maharaja of Mahishadal, a position Nirala himself filled briefly after his father's death in 1917. Thanks to the geographical accident of his birth Nirala grew up with Bengali as one of his two mother tongues, a circumstance which was to have important consequences for his development as a poet since it opened up to him the work of Tagore and the experimentation of younger writers in Calcutta. Baiswari was the language of his home and remained the medium of much of his familiar discourse and correspondence throughout his life.

In 1907 Nirala made his first journey to the family's ancestral home for his investiture with the sacred thread. Five years later he again returned to Kanauj for his betrothal to Manohradevi, an 11-year-old girl of Dalmau village. Two years later Nirala failed his high school matriculation examinations, for which his father banished him and sold or pawned Manohradevi's jewelry. The young couple returned to the bride's home in Dalmau, where both of Nirala's children were born, Ramakrishna in 1914 and Saroj in 1917.

Manohradevi apparently made Nirala aware of his deficiencies in *khaṛī bolī* and also first awakened him to the beauties of the poetry of Tulsi Das. Much of Nirala's education in Hindi was acquired during these years through studying back issues of periodicals like *Sarasvatī* and *Maryādā*.

To review Nirala's life is to confront a series of catastrophes, failures and losses that begins with the death of his mother when he was two. All this notwithstanding, by temperament Nirala was anything but lugubrious. The child in him was irrepressible; his pleasure in mystification (which had given him a reputation for sorcery among the women of Mahishadal), his love of play, the joy in flouting orthodoxy and a decided delight in battle for its own sake never deserted him. Even after his banishment from his father's house his main preoccupation seems to have been pranks and games. His carefree life ended with his father's death in 1917 and the loss of his wife, brother and sister-in-law in the influenza epidemic of 1918. He was left as the sole parent of not only Ramakrishna and Saroj but also the four of his brother's children who had survived. At twenty Nirala, seeking work to meet his heavy responsibilities, turned to the most unlikely career for the acquisition of wealth and became a poet.

After a short term in the Maharaja's service Nirala came to Calcutta and found a post as editor of the Ramakrishna Mission's periodical, *Samanvaya*. His two-year association with the Mission was no doubt of importance in directing him to a study of Vedanta, reflections of which are found throughout his work. In 1923 he became editor of a new journal, *Matvālā*, in which his first poems were published. During this time he became aware of Girishchandra Ghosh's Bengali plays in free verse and began at once to experiment himself with "mukt-chhand" in Hindi. In 1923 a small volume of his poems, including "*Juhī kī Kalī*" and "*Panchvaṭi-prasang*," appeared under the title *Anāmikā*. All these poems were republished in a much bigger volume in 1930 under the title *Parimal*.

At the time *Parimal* was published Nirala moved to Lucknow and spent most of the next twelve years there. This era saw the production of much of Nirala's finest work, including *Anāmikā* (a collection of poems that had nothing in common with the earlier volume of that name) and *Tulsī Dās*, along with several novels, short stories and essays. These were also years of uphill fighting against conservatives (both literary and social). The attacks on himself and his work often took the form of accusing him of insanity, characterizing his essays and poems as "the effusions of a diseased mind" and "the slaughter of literature."[4] With all his polemical activities Nirala filled these years with extraordinary labor, like the ones that followed in Allahabad. He was obliged to take on onerous editorial projects and an apparently endless series of hack translations to support his impoverished family. In 1935 his nineteen-year-old daughter died. His elegy for her, "*Saroj-smriti*," introduces a new note of unsparingly direct speech into his own art and Hindi literature in general, an intensely personal tone but objectively controlled, fusing the rhythmic flexibility of free verse with the solemn tread of classical meter. "*Saroj-smriti*" marked his full maturing as a poet.

Characteristically paradoxical, Nirala during the years following the death of Saroj produced such novels as the sunny comedy of *Nirupmā* and the ironic, hilarious and heart-breaking story of *Kullī Bhāt*. *Nirupmā* satirizes the wealthy Bengali society of Lucknow with the hero, a Kanyakubja Brahman like Nirala, at one point setting up as a shoe-shine boy to the immense discomfiture of the Brahman community. *Kullī Bhāt* is undisguisedly autobiographical and the source of much information on Nirala's marriage and early years. Both these novels mark a sophistication and subtlety of narrative technique that Hindi fiction since has not been able to match.

In the tales and essays of the thirties Nirala continued to "*épater les Brahmanes*," as it were, with satires of the cruelty and hypocrisy of certain pandits and with harangues on the decline of the various communities and the virtues of meat-eating. Nehru and Gandhiji were not spared. "Where is the Tagore of Hindi?" Gandhi had indiscreetly asked at the Sahitya Sammelan in Indore in 1936. He paid for it when he came to Lucknow where Nirala challenged him in public. To those who tried to bar his way saying, "Very important leaders are conferring with him," Nirala replied, "I'm an even more important poet," and pushed past them. After making Gandhi confess he did not know Hindi very well, Nirala said he would recite Tagore and his own work. Gandhi suggested that to save time it would be better if the poet sent him some of his books. An extraordinary scene, surely, and no less so was the one when Pandit Nehru found himself trapped in a railway carriage with the irate poet, who demanded to know why the regional assembly of which Nehru was president had not passed any resolution of regret over the recent deaths of Prasad and Premchand.[5]

During the Lucknow period and the last years in Allahabad, Nirala's life was marred by ill health, financial problems, and mental instability. Nirala led a simple, almost ascetic, existence although some recognition from beyond the immediate circle of his friends and disciples had begun to reach him. His fabled generosity insured his own continued poverty, and for his own good he was persuaded to leave his financial affairs in the hands of his long-time friend Mahadevi Verma. Accounts differ as to the nature (or even the reality) of his mental illness. Ramvilas Sharma denies that it could be termed a psychosis, calling it merely a "rather mild form of neurosis."[6] This is difficult to square with some of Nirala's letters and reported statements of the last years, with their extravagant claims to wealth and the friendship of famous people,[7] and his references to conversations with Queen Victoria or to his imaginary university degrees.[8] How much of all this was mere mystification can perhaps never be determined. During these years Nirala himself would say to people who came to call on him in Daraganj, "Nirala doesn't live here. The man you're looking for died long ago."[9]

What is certain is that his creative powers underwent no deterioration but rather continued to evolve; the last volumes, including the posthumously published *Sāndhya Kāklī*, contain some of his finest work.

The Poetry: The First Phase

The range of Nirala's poetry is far greater than that of any other twentieth-century Hindi poet. In the technical sphere he experimented with rhymed and unrhymed free verse, traditional meters, original stanza forms, ghazal, geet, bhajan, satire, long narrative, epic, elegy, and songs in folk style. He does not exclude Urdu or dialects from his vocabulary, unlike the other Chhayavadins, while in a poem like "*Rām kī Shakti Pūjā*" his language is as highly Sanskritized as Prasad's. The thematic spectrum ranges from the most intensely personal to the classically objective, from the mythic past to the present history of the Indian People.

The earliest of Nirala's poems to survive is "The *Juhī* Bud," in free verse irregularly rhymed. Nirala attributes its creation to the year 1916[10] but it was very likely written three or four years later; in any case, it is fully developed Chhayavad and one of the earliest poems of the type. The bud is described as a girl—"pure tender slender"—sleeping, "chilly in the folded leaf." Her lover, the wind, longing for her while far away in the mountains of the South, on an impulse returns to her in the night and awakens her. She

> started up,
> stared all about her, astonished,
> and found her darling by her bed.
> She smiled, gratified in her desire,
> and blossomed in her lover's arms.[11]

The personifications are not presented as fantasies or as conventional similes; the charm of the manner lies precisely in the combination of extravagant imagination and naive realism in human, dramatic terms. Although the poem offended some by its sensuousness, the intention is metaphysical in the Chhayavad way. As in the early Upanishads the daring of the analogy serves to underscore the belief in the fundamental unity of all things in the natural universe. Compared to the Absolute, nature may have only a qualified reality, but one that is not without significance since it manifests the Absolute.

This is not to say that Nirala does not revel in the physical beauties of the world for their own sake. He does, indeed, with a passion that makes the other Chhayavadins appear bloodless. His conception of the natural universe in these poems is fundamentally erotic. The holy surge of the seasons, the rise and decline of vegetation, the powers of wind and storm, even the fixed revolution of night and day, all testify to the sovereignty of Kama. The basic metaphor is actually the technique itself, by means of which Nirala sports in the virtuosity of a liberated new poetic diction disciplined only by the intrinsic demands of the subject while he rides roughshod over all the traditional restraints of both prudish decorum and worn-out rules of conventional prosody. In this lies the real freedom of Nirala's free verse. The personal and humanistic feeling for nature, to be expressed in poems such as "*Van-Belā*" ("Wild Jasmine"), was still several years away.

In "*Panchvaṭi-prasang*" Nirala offers his first poetic treatment of a part of the Ramayana in the form of five dramatic fragments. Here he explicitly states some of his Advaita (non-dualist) philosophical convictions:

> There's only One; no second's there at all.
> The sense of Two is the only error.
> And all the same, beloved,
> from the very heart of error
> we must rise and pass beyond it.[12]

To Lakshmana's question as to how the world is continually recreated, Rama answers:

> Those who through desire take body in this world,
> their souls depart and come again
> and their desire creates ever new creations.[13]

Here breathes the very spirit of the early Upanishads. But significantly Lakshmana, as though looking ahead to the later Upanishads and the Gita, says that "service is the one recourse of life:"

I know not liberation, but devotion alone,
and it is enough.[14]

At the conclusion of *Parimal,* in a poem entitled "Awakening," the Upanishads are invoked and quoted as the source of salvation:

> The free door was opened
> forever for the giving
> of the great teaching to the world:
> "*Tat tvam asi.*"

And the poet, shedding ego and grief, proclaims

> Restraints and limits broken,
> the gross body cast off. . . .

and holds up the ideal of a simple language to express the "word-born world," free of adjectives and without a trace of *alankār* or paronomasia,

> . . . plain as the naked blue sky
> even today in the preserved language of the Vedas,
> the verse free,
> the natural expression of the heart.[15]

Not all of *Parimal* is in the exalted Vedantic mode. In "Beggar" Nirala gives an unforgettable realistic portrait of the Indian mendicant with "his heart in two pieces, his belly and back in one."[16]

In one of the many poems entitled "*Bādal Rāg*" ("Cloud Music") Nirala hails the storm as the symbol of the revolution to come, pointing out that only the humble, like the plants in the fields, "take a beauty from the storm." And while the rich man, even in his beloved's embrace, trembles to hear the thunder,

> the anguished peasant calls to you,
> you heroes of the storm-clouds.
> They've sucked his juices dry,
> he stands mere bones,
> oh life-redeeming storm.[17]

In one of the two poems titled "Waken Once Again" (1921) he gives the first of many expressions of nationalist sentiment to be found throughout his work:

> In the lions' lair today
> the jackals have moved in.
> Who can snatch the cub from the
>   shelter of the lioness?
> Is she silent so long as life is in her?
> Fools!

Only a sheep-mother
stands by unblinking
when her offspring are carried off.
. . . . .
But the able and worthy people will prevail—
this is no saying of the West
but the Gita, the Gita.[18]

Parimal is a rich and varied volume. Nirala's first great elegy,
"*Yamunā ke Prati,*" is there, singing the death of the Braj tradition,
the end, for a time at least, of Krishna's sovereignty. There are also
other poems of social protest, like "The Widow," and metaphysical
nature poems such as "To the Flower by the Wayside" conceived in
a spirit and tone that recall Herrick. Above all, in poem after poem
Nirala calls for the spontaneous flow of feeling, the joyful response to
impulse, letting go, as in "The Stream":

Let it flow—
Obstacles can never stop it.
Who's ever seen
The flooded river of wild youth
Turned from its course?[19]

or in "To a Waterfall," where the mountain stream, "in love with
darkness," tumbles and rushes on, its music resounding within the
heart of the very stone that tries in vain to stop it—a metaphor, surely,
for Nirala's own poetic art.[20]

Gītikā (1936) is Nirala's next collection. Here the poet turns away,
for the most part, from the objective world and treats the subject of
love metaphysically in a series of a hundred and one brief lyrics, so
compressed, so dependent on every kind of musical effect as to be
virtually untranslatable.

Lover, the night has wakened.
Her drowsy eyes, half-closed lotuses,
yearn for her young lover's sun-bright face.

The splendor of her loosened hair
floats over neck shoulders arms and breasts,
making her glance another sun
lurking behind the clouds,
its rays her bright limbs.
Outdone, the lightning flash
craves her forgiveness.

Covering her breast, she tosses her hair behind her,

stares all around her and walks with a swan's grace.
In her house she is
the victory garland of her husband's love:
unburdened of desire, a pearl
sewn with the thread of renunciation.[21]

It is at first impossible to say whether night is being described in terms of the *nāyikā* or the reverse, so complete is the fusion of the two components of the analogy. Like English metaphysical poetry of the seventeenth century, this song is full of paradoxes (the wakening of the night, the mysterious relationship of renunciation and fulfillment). The music of assonance and internal rhyme will be apparent from the Hindi of the opening lines:

(priya) yāminī jāgī.
alas pankaj-drig arun-mukh-
tarun-anurāgī.

In the last line of the poem the effect is partly achieved through punning (another popular seventeenth-century device)—*mukti* (liberation) and *muktā* (pearl), *tyāg* (renunciation) and *tāgī* (sewn).

Not all the poems of *Gītikā* are so complicated, so close to preciousness; many, in fact, have the directness of folk song. But it is worth noting that even with the first edition of the volume it was felt necessary to append explanatory notes, notes which later commentaries sometimes ignore.[22]

Anāmikā, Nirala's most consistently impressive collection, was published in 1938. It contains two of Nirala's three great long poems, "*Saroj-smriti*" and "*Rām kī Shakti-Pūjā*." The writing here is characterized by a greater daring of imagination and language along with a much franker preoccupation with the actual circumstances of the poet's own life. The language is apt to shift with ease from the most recondite Sanskritized diction to statements of the utmost simplicity—a trait not found among the other Chhayavadins.

In the long poem "*Van-Belā*" ("Wild Jasmine") Nirala reviews his whole career and concludes:

My life's a total waste.
I've lost the battle.[23]

He reflects that if he had been some maharaja's son he'd have been pampered, flattered and sent off to an English university to carouse with lordlings, while his father, keeping firm control over his wealth, would also follow the fashion by posing as a Communist and preaching revolution. Then with the sudden realization that he is not alone but surrounded by the "smiling jasmine," Nirala changes his tone as he imagines a metaphysical dialogue with the bloming vine, which tells him:

> "Only yourself you've wasted, only played
> in this life . . ."[24]

and stirs his old idealism to new life:

> On your stem,
> when under the wild beating of the hail,
> you dance.[25]

In this stylistically and emotionally varied poem Nirala makes the shifts with apparent ease from the opening description of the world at spring, which is conventionally Chhayavad for all its brilliance, to the autobiographical musings that follow, and then in turn to the malicious satire of his reflections on national politics and society (not sparing even the Hindi academicians), and finally to the exquisite but always disciplined conversation with the wild jasmine, whimsical but devoid of sentimentality, serene and moving in a way to equal the passages on flowers in *The Winter's Tale.*

"*Saroj-smriti,*" the elegy Nirala wrote for his daughter in 1935, also evokes the late Shakespearean romances, for Saroj is a Perdita who is not recovered, a Marina who does not survive, but whose life nevertheless redeems her father's. The poem, embodying Nirala's grief and self-reproach at the death of his daughter at 19, moves far beyond the frontiers of Chhayavad. In 159 rhymed couplets Nirala sums up his life, his frustrations as a writer, his failure as a provider for his family, and his rebellion against orthodox society. The emotional range of the poem is enormous, encompassing despair, hilarity, tenderness, exultation, bitter sarcasm, and resignation, all magnificently controlled by the rigorous discipline of the form. At the climax of the poem, at her wedding, Saroj appears to him as another Shakuntala, only with

> a different lesson, and a different art.[26]

The lesson and the art were to provide the basis for Nirala's own finest achievements. For although he says in his grief,

> how can I tell it now
> when I could not before?[27]

it is with the poignant directness of statement of "*Saroj-smriti*" that Nirala's art reaches its highest development.

"*Rām kī Shakti-Pūjā*" (1936) is a tour de force of quite another order, a highly Sanskritized epic fragment based on the Puranic tradition, found in the *Devi Bhāgavata* but in neither Valmiki nor Tulsi, that recounts how Rama rises from despair to triumph over Ravana by performing a ritual worship of Shakti. The poem is a fusion of Vaishanava and Shaiva traditions, of Nirala's devotion to Tulsi and the impress on him of his early association with the Shri Ramakrishna Mission in Calcutta. In offering his sacrifice to Shakti, Rama finds that one lotus is lacking; in desperation he addresses the absent Sita:

> A curse on a life that's only struggle,
> A curse on the faith for which I've always sacrificed.[28]

Then he remembers that when he was a child, Kausalya had called him "lotus-eyed" and he is about to offer up his eye when the Goddess intervenes, entering into him and symbolically assuring his victory over Ravana, who had been her devotee. "*Rām kī Shakti-Pūjā*" is not only a combination of epic and mysticism; it is also, and perhaps above all, an allegory of Nirala's own career.

Among the poems in *Anāmikā* there are also realistic portraits, more controlled but no less emotional than "Beggar." In "Breaking Stones" Nirala describes a young woman laboring "on a road in Allahabad"; admiration for her toughness and beauty rather than conventional pathos provides the dominant tone and another instance of Nirala's originality of approach. In "Giving" the poet, on a morning stroll, admiring the beauties of spring, observes a Brahman feeding monkeys on a Lucknow bridge while a skeletal beggar gets only curses.

In 1938 Nirala also published his longest poem, *Tulsī Dās*. As "*Rām kī Shakti-Pujā*" had shown us Nirala as Rama, here he appears as Tulsi, always one of his favorite poets. The well-known (if partly legendary) circumstances of Tulsi's early life, his visions and the rejection by Ratnavali, his wife, which turns him finally to devotional poetry, are recounted in one hundred six-line stanzas. The background is the sunset of the old Hindu civilization and the alluring but destructive moonrise of the Mughal way of life. Tulsi's integrity and devotion, enshrined in his art, will serve to guide India during the long night and remind her of her ideal greatness. Nirala no doubt means to suggest the parallels between Tulsi's life during the Mughal domination with his own in what was to be the last decade of the Raj.

The Middle Years

In *Kukurmuttā* (*Mushroom*) (1942) Nirala presents a satirical fable in rhymed free verse. Coming after *Anāmikā* and *Tulsī Dās*, this *divertissement* suggests a temporary decline in the poet's inspiration, a probably necessary pause for breath before the last great period. The mushroom —Indian, spontaneously arisen and edible—maintains its superiority over the beautiful but useless imported rose. Indian critics have never reached any consensus on the intention of the work.[29] Rose and mushroom: capitalist and socialist, politician and poor man, Pant and Nirala? The tone is so fantastical, its range so wide, that unanimity of interpretation would be difficult to achieve. Nirala is very likely poking fun at himself, along with everyone else, when he has the mushroom claim sovereignty in the world of forms because everything from Vishnu's discus and the royal umbrella to the dome and the parachute is modeled on it. The lines usually interpreted as an attack on T. S. Eliot apply at least as much to his Indian imitators:

> As T. S. Eliot tossed out
> A stone from here, a pebble from there
> His readers, with their hands on their hearts,
> Exclaimed, "He's described the whole world!"[30]

Where the poem has real success is in the suddenly serious description of the dilapidated stinking huts of the poor that lie just outside the Navab's splendid garden.[31]

Although *Animā* (1943), the next collection, returns in part to the mystical themes of *Gītikā*, the diction is generally simpler and the emotion more convincing. High seriousness is no longer immune to humor.

> I know I've crossed
> The rivers and torrents I had to cross.
> I laugh now as I see
> There wasn't any boat.[32]

The next collection in order of composition, *Naye Patte* (March, 1946), published after *Belā* (January, 1946), contains much of Nirala's writing of the war years. The satirical and stylistically colloquial intention of *Kukurmuttā* is here carried out with greater success. Most of the poems are humorous or bitterly ironic. The main exception is an ode to Saraswati of Keatsian richness of concrete detail, with realistic and affectionate evocations of the seasons and village life.

The satire can be gentle or fierce. In "Hot Pakoras" a gourmand laments that he has given up the Brahman's cooking for the savory, tongue-burning pakoras. A Brahman boy in "Love Song" tells of his love for a Kahar girl, "black as a cuckoo," for whom he bides his time.[33] The humble pilgrim of "*Sphatik-Shilā*" sees a girl bathing in a stream,

> The wet dhoti clinging tight to her body,
> breasts firm and lovely, stirring up a sinner's heart,

and concludes:

> I thought of Sita
> And said, "You wife of Ram,
> What a vision you've given me!"[34]

This is the most spiritual *darshan* he gets on his pilgrimage.

The political satire is less amiable. Mr. Gidwani of "Moscow Dialogues," "my new friend and a very important socialist," boasts of how he has acquired the Moscow Dialogues from Subhash Bose in prison, then complains:

> "I've no time for anything.
> My elder brother's building a bungalow
> And I'm in charge . . .
> By the way, I've written a novel.
> Have a look at it, won't you?"

Mr. Gidwani's novel begins, "I adore that dear Shyama who doesn't requite my love. . ." "Then," Nirala says, "I looked at the 'Moscow Dialogues' and then at Mr. Gidwani."[35]

In "Mahngu" Pandit Nehru—"London graduate, M. A. and barrister"—comes in his motor car to visit a village while his wife, we are reminded, is in Switzerland for her health. Nehru appeals to the people for support in the elections; soon they'll have their freedom. Lukua, a simple peasant, unable to understand Panditji, asks his friend Mahngu for his opinion. Mahngu explains that the Congress leaders are actually the friends of the mill owners and foreigners, not of the villagers. "But we're many," Mahngu says, "hidden, our names are not printed in the papers."

> "The country will be free,
> The poet wrote, so long as you don't change.
> I've told myself, 'I'm Mahngu,
> And even if the earth under my feet goes
>   flying to the skies,
> Still I'll never change,
> That's how high my price will be.' "[36]

The language throughout *Naye Patte* is plain, colloquial, idiomatic. It still remained for Nirala to fuse this down-to-earth manner with the serious poetry of the last four volumes and thereby to achieve a revolution in Hindi poetry comparable to that of Eliot and Yeats in English.

Belā is a collection of different kinds of songs in "simple, idiomatic language," as Nirala says in his foreword.[37] There are several experiments with ghazal in both conventional Hindi and in a mixture of Hindi and Urdu, along with adaptations of traditional Urdu meters, all calculated to disturb the purists. The subject of most of the songs is love, both metaphysical and erotic, but there are patriotic and satirical pieces, with more attacks on Nehru and the privileged classes. The chief significance of *Belā* is that it served as an experiment for Nirala in his attempts to create a metaphysical poetry that would transcend the limitations of the earlier poems in this vein, an experiment that culminated in the perfectly realized devotional songs of the next four, the final, volumes of the poet's work.

The Final Period

Archnā (1950), *Ārādhnā* (1953), *Git Gunj* (1954; expanded edition in 1959), and the posthumously published *Sāndhya Kākli* (1969) constitute a generally unified series of short lyrics. Despite their brevity and surface simplicity they are also the poet's final testament, his late quartets, his ultimate withering into the truth. The predominant *rasas* are *adbhuta*, *karunā* and *shānta*.[38]   Living alone in Daraganj, ill and bitterly disappointed in the new, free India, Nirala renounces the world of politics along with society to turn to a prolonged meditation on his own personal relationship with the wider world of the spirit. In so doing he reestablishes his bond with the bhakti poets of the sixteenth and seventeenth centuries but always on his own highly individual and original terms. Despite the outer circumstances of his life the tone of the lyrics is most often positive, sometimes exuberant; it is also occasionally, especially in the final volume, obscure (perhaps because even here Nirala continued to experiment). But the prevailing sanity of the poems is manifest. Whatever the truth of Nirala's mental condition during the last decade of his life, these poems offer a convincing argument for the continuing strength and clarity of his mind.

The seemingly artless poems of these final volumes are the most difficult of all Nirala's works to translate. Their substance inheres in the now chastened Hindi, the humble idioms expressing the high concept, and in the objectification of a universe so entirely private that no distinction is made between the personal and the general, and in fact need not be made since such a distinction is held to be in any case illusory. The "I," "you," "we," and "they" of these songs are all Nirala and everybody else at once. Consider:

> Whoever's spent
> these days of sorrow
> counting and counting
> the minutes, the trifles,
> has strung a necklace
> of tears like pearls
> and tossed it around
> his lover's throat
> to see the fair face
> serene and bright,
> in the night of sorrow.[39]

Or:

> The heart's affection drawn to you,
> suffused fragrance of the world's desire;
> freedom won from the pure
> Ganges stream, the Kashi of the mind.[40]

To illustrate the difficulties of translating, in the four-line stanza, for example, the Hindi consists of eight-syllable lines, unencumbered with articles, and depending on the most commonplace idioms to do the work of the clumsy and rather high-toned English participles "drawn" and "won."

Though the devotional mood predominates in these last volumes, there are several poems that are objective and earthy. Nirala's great love of the rains is reflected in several songs, and there are genre descriptions of village life.

> There are mangoes and roseapples,
> some figs and unripe *gullu;*
> the boys go wild picking them out—
> there are real ones on every tree.
> Then the oldest son's wife
> sets out the little sweet cakes
> and gets Manni to cook them.[41]

This kind of evocation suggests Elizabethan genre descriptions where, as here, the simple concrete detail (including the one proper name) is all. So too with this description of a garden:

Flower garden
like
a fragrant sari.

> Bejeweled with blooms.
> rooted vines climbing,
> billowing west wind,
> flowing channels.

> Shall I say,
> a mist has spread?
> The garden flickers
> with dusky melons
> and beds of gourds.[42]

With some license the initial simile could also be read: "Fragrant sari like a garden," but Nirala's intention seems to be rather to avoid this more conventional figure and instead to suggest the ways the actual world of nature is like its representation through artifice.

In Nirala's final collection, *Sāndhya Kākli (Evening Song)*, there are more evocations of the seasons and the rains characterized by an ultimate simplicity in which the music and allusiveness of the Hindi are more important than ever in his work.

> Fresh clouds cover the black sky,
> spread over forests, mountains, gardens, faces.[43]

A comparison with these lines in Hindi reveals the musical art of this apparent artlessness:

> shyām gagan nav ghan mandalāye
> kānan-giri-van-ānan chhāye.

The onomatopoeia and the internal rhymings are completely unforced and wonderfully evoke the cooling rain, while "*shyām*," blue-black, is also a standard epithet for Krishna, who throughout the Uttar Pradesh and Bengal is so thoroughly associated with the monsoon.

Most moving of the poems in *Sāndhya Kākli* are those in which Nirala turns to speak for the last time of his own life and career, as in the final poem of the volume, undated but very possibly the last he wrote:

> The ending of the play—a flowering
> whether it bore fruit
> or withered barren,
> a holy sage's on a bed of leaves
> or just some ordinary man's.
> Bhishma
> on the cruel bed of arrows
> turns his gaze upwards.[44]

The comparison with Bhishma, the warrior-sage of the Mahabharata, is not made lightly. Nirala too was the preceptor of a generation, a fighter and uncompromising idealist. Like Bhishma dying on his bed of arrows, at the end of his life Nirala takes a last look upwards; *Sāndhya Kākli* represents that final vision. The poem is a fitting coda to the great career that had preceded it, neither a holy sage's nor an ordinary man's, but a poet's. The significance of that career is perhaps most succinctly expressed by Nirala himself in some lines from the elegy he wrote in 1940 for Jayshankar Prasad:

> You made even the monkey beautiful,
> turned the mute eloquent, took a little and gave much more,
> drank poison but made the people's literature immortal.[45]

The Translation

Nirala's Hindi is subtle, flexible and individual. As regards vocabulary he draws not only from the immense treasure of Sanskrit, with its vast numbers of synonyms and near-synonyms, but also from the Persian and Arabic reserves of Urdu and even occasionally from local dialects such as his native Baiswari. In his inventive compoundings, richness of musical effect and allusiveness, and intricacy of syntax Nirala may justly be compared with Hopkins in English.

Among the general characteristics of Hindi that might be pointed out are the absence of articles, a great freedom of participial construction, and sufficient inflection to allow a freer word order and more frequent omission of pronouns than are possible in English or French though rather less than in Latin. Nirala makes the most of all the possibilities of the language for flexibility, heightened effects from unexpected word order, pronominal ambiguity, and the like. The difficulties of his work led some contemporary critics to declare him insane, and some of his poems continue to baffle readers. Ambiguity is central to his technique and a not surprising concomitant in a poet of such originality. The ambiguities are not those of an imperfect craft but result from the impulse to express a new vision that must synthesize, transform and even annihilate existing conventions.

In addition to the general difficulties of Nirala's style and thought there are those of variations in different printings of the poems. The translator, or for that matter, the Hindi-speaking reader, of Nirala is constantly brought up against not only the frequent obvious typographical errors but important discrepancies in words, punctuation, hyphenization (so important in a style where a whole verse or more may be made up of one or more groups of compounded nouns), and even in separation into strophe or section. This is particularly true of the poems from *Anāmikā*, including the important long poems "*Van-Belā*" (*Wild Jasmine*) and "*Saroj-smriti*" (*Remembering Saroj*), often so difficult in any case because of the compression of the language and the unpredictable freedom of invention. Since even Hindi authorities differ in their interpretations and base them on differing printings, the translator must obviously rely ultimately on his own judgment.

In making these translations I have used for the most part a free or accentual verse, occasionally blank verse, and generally avoided rhyme. My intention has been to keep as close to the original as was possible, sinning if need be on the side of literalness. The "interpreted" translation or "transcreation" has always seemed to me an unnecessary accommodation to the rarity (until recently) of scholars with sufficient command of both English and Hindi to do the work as ultimately it must be done—by one person with one mind and one temperament, instead of resorting to a sort of committee of experts on various phases of the work.

Modern Hindi poetry has been best known in America and England in V. N. Misra's *Modern Hindi Poetry: An Anthology*. The versions given there are "transcreations," productions of American poets who know no Hindi working from versions produced by Hindi poets and scholars. The resulting "translations," no matter how interesting they may be in their own right (and that of course varies enormously depending on the American poet), are often so far from the original that their authors would be hard put to recognize them. Of the six Nirala poems included in the Misra collection I have translated only three here. For purposes of comparison here are the last three lines of M. Halpern's transcreation of "A Stump," of which a very literal version will be found in this volume.

> No lover weeps in the spot of shade
> Cast by an old blind bird who sits there
> Dumbly recalling the music it once could make.[46]

It will be seen from this how liberal the transcreators can be, changing the number of lovers, connecting the first and second lines (which are stanzaically separated in the Hindi, the first line ending with a full stop) and thus establishing an emotional relation which is entirely new, and qualifying the bird as "blind" and "dumb" and his memories as sentimentally specific in a way utterly alien to Nirala's simple direct-ness. In the case of "At the Landing"[47] the transcreation converts the village to a town and invents "wavelets" to prettify the scene. The version of "To a Waterfall"[48] is not a translation at all but a new poem which seems to incorporate some faulty memories of the original. Since the main qualities of poems like "A Stump" and the untitled poem the transcreators call "At the Landing" are terseness and the absence of conventional romantic or sensuous imagery, it seems reasonable to expect the translator (whatever he may call himself) to convey some impression of these qualities. I do not believe that what is involved here is solely a matter of taste or problems of reconstruction imposed by the task of transferring the poetry from one language (and culture) to another. The translator must be guided by a principle of maximum fidelity and at the least suggest the original if he cannot recreate it. It has seemed to me, in any case, that very often a simple and literal rendering may have more eloquence and poetic intensity in English than any of the elaborate improvisations on the original poem to which the transcreators so often resort.

The selection of poems from Nirala's very large output has been dictated in part by the accessibility of the poem's subject matter or theme to a non-Indian audience. With the exception of *Tulsī Dās* all the volumes of Nirala's verse are represented here.[49] The extended nar-rative of *Tulsī Dās* does not lend itself to excerption, and nothing less than a complete translation could do the work justice. All the poems included here, apart from the selection from *Kukurmuttā*, are complete.

It is my hope that this book will encourage others to explore the riches of Nirala's work (including his prose) as well as that of the other great writers of the twentieth-century Hindi renaissance, who so genuinely deserve to be known in the West.

SOURCES OF THE POEMS

(Untitled poems are indicated by their first lines.)

Parimal: Only One Madness; Poem; River Crossing; Cloud Music; Beggar; In the Forest of Panchvati; The *Juhī* Bud; To a Waterfall; Done; To the Flower by the Wayside; Recognized; First Dawn; Paradise; A Solution; Eyes.

Gītikā:	Lover, the night has wakened; Because, my dear, I love him; Shedding its last rays the sun.
Anāmikā:	To a Friend; It's True; Letter to the Flowers of Hindi; Hopeless; A Stump; A Look at Death; Wild Jasmine; Breaking Stones; Giving; To Love; Misunderstanding; Consoled; Clear Skies; Remembering Saroj.
Animā:	The stream of love has run dry; Have mercy Lord; I'm Alone.
Bela:	Don't see yourself as alien.
Naye Patte:	Blood Holi; Love Song.
Kukurmuttā:	Outside the garden lay the huts.
Archnā:	Don't tie the boat up here, friend; What opens will decline; Dense darkness shrouds the earth; Why have you forgotten me; Make all things natural; Whoever's spent; The cuckoo speaks in every grove; At the touch of my lover's hand I woke; Every thread was worn out; Guide the ship; With sweetest tones you called.
Ārādhnā:	A little boat; Plowing done the team comes home; Flower garden; Let me walk the straight path;* Body broken, mind sick;* Where man's no better than a horse or ox.*
Git Gunj:	Beneficent our honored Sharda.
Sāndhya Kāklī:	Fresh clouds cover the black sky; Shining autumn fills the skies; The buds have come back to the jasmine; The poison of a life.

* Also published in *Git Gunj.*

Notes

NOTES TO THE POEMS

P.15* The friend was Umashankar Bajpeyi, a poet and critic of Chhayavad, who still wrote in Braj and followed the conventions Nirala had discarded.

15 ** The various "Malhar" *rāgs* are associated with the rainy season.

15 *** Traditional enemies.

16 * The "pancham," fifth degree of the Indian scale, is identified with assertiveness and affirmation.

18 * A pun on "*ashok*" (the tree) and "*a-shok*" (without grief.).

19 * "*Muktā*" (pearl) conventionally evokes "*mukti*" (liberation or salvation) in Chhayavad poetry. The creation of the pearl as a metaphor for the artist creating poetry from his suffering, is a frequent figure in Urdu poetry.

19 ** Goddess of the arts and learning.

21 * For *flower* Nirala uses "*suman*," which is also an archaic term for god or godling.

22 * The rhyme in Hindi parallels the English:
        "Na dekhā usmen kabhī vishād, dekhā sirf ek unmād."

28 * Interested readers may wish to compare this fairly literal translation with the transcreation on p. 88 of Misra's *Modern Hindi Poetry.*

32 * The papiha's song is heard by Nirala as "*Pi kahan?*" ("Lover where?"). It is associated with love's longing and the separation of lovers in the rains. The koel, the Indian cuckoo, is often identified with spring and the awakening of new love.

38 *I.e., over the common people.

38 ** "*jalaj*," "born of the water."

38 *** "*ruddh kosh, hay kshubd tosh*," literally "treasure blocked up, gratification is tormented."

39 * Abhimanyu was the heroic son of Arjuna who died young in the battle of the Kauravas and Pandavas.

43 * So that the monkeys would report it to Hanuman, who would then intercede for him with Lord Rama.

47 * A very low-caste community whose members traditionally do such menial tasks as drawing water from the wells.

49 * In the original the only pronominal expression is "your." Some Indian commentators paraphrase the second and third stanzas using "my" and "me," but Nirala's deliberate avoidance of such words makes plain his wish that the prayer be construed as universal, not personal.

53 * Celestial musicians.

54 * Wife of the sage Atri at Chitrakut, where the exiles had stopped on their wanderings.

55 * Lal is a term of affection, Lakhan a dialect form of Lakshmana.

55 ** Parashurama was a Brahman and also an incarnation of Vishnu who attempted to extirpate the warrior cast (Kshatriyas).

55 *** When Rama's brother Bharat, who was ruling in his stead, came to visit him in exile Lakshmana mistakenly thought he had come to attack them.

57 * A bird believed to live by drinking moonbeams.

57 ** A Himalayan lake, according to legend the source of the Ganges.

59 * Represented as having a fish or crocodile on his banner.

60 * Maya.

60 ** Yoga.

62 * The three basic elements of Nature, according to the Sankhya system, approximately spirit, passion and ignorance.

63 * Like Krishna, Rama is usually portrayed as dark blue.

73 * There are puns on *mukti* (liberation) and *muktā* (pearl), *tāgī* (sewn) and *tyāg* (renunciation).

74 * The form of address in this and the next poem is *"sakhi,"* an archaism used exclusively by women speaking to other women.

76 * An evening *rāg* associated with the rains and the separation of lovers.

77 * A very free rendering of the last two lines. The original alludes to technical terms of Sanskrit and Hindi prosody.

78 * Goddess of the dawn.

91 * *Sasu*—mother-in-law (Saroj's maternal grandmother); throughout the poem Nirala refers to her as Sasu or Sasuji.

91 ** Under the influence of Mangal (Mercury), thought to be unlucky. A "mangali" in any case should marry only another "mangali."

92 * A midnight *rāg*. In the tradition of Indian music a new instrument is preferred to an old one.

92 * A pun, *"bahār"* meaning spring, and by extension exuberance, and also a springtime *rāg*.

93 * Nirala's community, Brahmans from Kanauj, whom Nirala often attacks for their orthodoxy and arrogance.

94 * Normally a marriage would depend on the astrologers' interpretations of the horoscopes of bride and groom. Conflicting charts would oblige the parents of both parties to seek new matches.

95 * Goddess of desire and spouse of Kama, the Indian Eros.

95 ** The poet, renouncing his work in this life as a failure, offers Saroj, as the traditional sacrifice to the deceased relation, whatever merit he may have acquired in previous lives, i.e., the most precious spiritual possession anyone may have.

102 * To make the soup-like *dal* the gram or pulse must split out of its husk, whence the Hindi idiom to indicate success after difficulty. In this poem the husk of the gram suggests a metaphor for the intact ego which must be shed for salvation. This fusion of the gnomic and colloquial characterizes many of the poems of Nirala's last volumes and provides a major source of difficulty in their translation.

105 * An image from Vedic literature: the arrow pierces the darkness to bring light, the cloud to bring rain, etc.

108 * *Nyctanthes arbor tristis*, shephalika or har-singar (love-stealing). The dye from the blossoms is used for Buddhist robes, which may contribute to the plant's generally melancholy connotation.

116 * The berry-like fruit of the mahua (*bassia latifolia*).

118 * Sharda is another name for Sarasvati, goddess of learning and the arts. Her festival is celebrated on Vasant Panchami, usually in February. Nirala was born on Vasant Panchami.

119 * August 15 is Indian Independence Day.

NOTES TO THE AFTERWORD

1. *Sāket* and *Yashodhara*, Maithili Sharan's finest works, were both published in 1932.

2. *Hindī Sāhitya Kosh* (Banaras, 1963), v. 1, p. 325.

3. Most sources give 1896 or 1897 but Ramvilas Sharma, in his excellent biography, *Nirālā kī Sāhitya Sādhnā* (Delhi, 1969), makes out a convincing case for 1899. See pp. 490–7 for a full discussion of this question, as also of the problem of the dating of "*Juhī kī Kalī*" and Pant's priority in developing free verse.

4. Quoted in Sharma, *op. cit.*, p. 201.

5. Nirala, *Prabandh-Pratimā* (Allahabad, 1940), pp. 18–34.

6. Sharma, *op. cit.*, p. 512.

7. *Ibid.*, p. 511.

8. *Ibid.*, p. 429.

9. *Ibid.*, p. 442.

10. See Sharma, *op. cit.*, pp. 491–3.

11. Nirala, *Parimal* (Lucknow, 1966), pp. 171–2.

12. *Ibid.*, p. 230.

13. *Ibid.*, p. 229.

14. *Ibid.*, pp. 219–20.

15. *Ibid.*, pp. 238–42.

16. *Ibid.*, p. 125. (In current printings of *Parimal* the last three lines of the poem have been omitted.)

17. *Ibid.*, pp. 166–7.

18. *Ibid.*, pp. 180–1.

19. *Ibid.*, p. 134.

20. *Ibid.*, p. 153.

21. Nirala, *Gītikā* (Allahabad, 1936), p. 4.

22. For example, most glosses ignore the hyphen at the end of the poem's second line and attribute the sun-bright face to the *nayika* herself.

23. Nirala, *Anāmikā* (Allahabad, 1963), p. 86.

24. *Ibid.*, p. 91.

25. *Ibid.*, p. 93.

26. *Ibid.*, p. 137.

27. *Ibid.*

28. *Ibid.*, p. 167.

29. For a discussion of Indian opinion of *Kukurmuttā* see Krishnadev Jhari, *Yugkavi Nirālā* (New Delhi, 1970), pp. 52–3.

30. Nirala, *Kukurmuttā* (Allahabad, 1969), p. 46.

31. *Ibid.*, pp. 49–50, translated here on p. 48.

32. Nirala, *Animā* (Allahabad, 1971), p. 12.

33. Nirala, *Naye Patte* (Allahabad, 1962), pp. 46–7.

34. *Ibid.*, pp. 59–60.

35. *Ibid.*, pp. 25–6.

36. *Ibid.*, pp. 106–10.

37. Nirala, *Belā* (Allahabad, 1962), p. 5.

38. Roughly, the wonderful, the compassionate and the serene.

39. Nirala, *Archnā* (Allahabad, 1962), p. 78.

40. Nirala, *Ārādhnā* (Allahabad, 1963), p. 50.

41. *Ibid.*, p. 74.

42. *Ibid.*, p. 75.

43. Nirala, *Sāndhya Kāklī* (Allahabad, 1969), p. 18.

44. *Ibid.*, p. 87.

45. *Animā*, p. 18.

46. *Modern Hindi Poetry: An Anthology,* ed. V. N. Misra (Bloomington, 1965), p. 69.

47. *Ibid.*, p. 97, translated here on p. 26.

48. *Ibid.*, p. 34, translated here on p. 72.

49. The volume entitled *Aparā* is itself an anthology, made by Nirala in 1950, and contains nothing not previously published in other collections.